SPORTS HEROES AND LEGENDS™

Tim
Duncan

Read all of the books in this exciting, action-packed biography series!

Barry Bonds

Ichiro Suzuki

Lou Gehrig

Michelle Kwan

Mickey Mantle

Tim Duncan

Tim Duncan

by Sean Adams

LERNER
SPORTS
AN IMPRINT OF LERNER PUBLISHING GROUP

For Dennis Dalelio, our favorite "good guy"

LernerSports
An imprint of Lerner Publishing Group
241 First Avenue North
Minneapolis, MN 55401 U.S.A.

Website address: www.lernerbooks.com

Cover photograph:
© JP Thomas/Panoramic/Zuma Press

Library of Congress Cataloging-in-Publication Data

Adams, Sean, 1977–
        Tim Duncan / by Sean Adams.
        p. cm.— (Sports heroes and legends)
        Includes bibliographical references and index.
        Contents: In the Spotlight—A rough start—Coming to America—Sophomore superstar—Number one—Texas Titans—On the brink—Slam Duncan—Most valuable person—Fast break—A perfect moment—One of the good guys.
        ISBN: 0–8225–1793–0 (lib. bdg. : alk. paper)
        1. Duncan, Tim, 1976– —Juvenile literature. 2. Basketball players—United States—Biography—Juvenile literature. [1. Duncan, Tim, 1976– 2. Basketball players.] I. Title. II. Series.
        GV884.D86A65 2004
        796.323′092—dc22   2003026216

Manufactured in the United States of America
1 2 3 4 5 6 – JR – 09 08 07 06 05 04

Contents

In the Spotlight

I've been here before, Tim Duncan told himself as he warmed up with the rest of the Wake Forest University basketball squad. *It's just like last year.*

In 1995, as a college sophomore, Tim had poured in sixteen points and contributed twenty rebounds to an 82–80 Wake Forest victory in the Atlantic Coast Conference (ACC) championship game. Wake Forest's Demon Deacons dramatically beat the University of North Carolina (UNC) Tar Heels. The upset had given Wake Forest its first ACC title in thirty-three years and brought the team major attention. Tim could still remember the amazing rush he'd felt when the final buzzer sounded, and he tried to pump up his confidence that he could repeat that moment.

But there was one major difference between the game Tim was about to play in and the match he'd helped his team win the previous year. Last time he'd been a supporting player, backing up Wake Forest's star Randolph Childress as Childress won the game with a basket in the last seconds.

This year Childress wasn't around anymore. He was playing professionally for the Portland Trail Blazers in the National Basketball Association (NBA), leaving Tim to take over the lead role. Tim sure hoped he was up to the challenge. It had been fourteen years since any team in the ACC had won back-to-back championships, and he was eager to break the streak.

Of course, the only way to do that was out on the court . . . and before he knew it, it was time for the opening tip-off against opposing team Georgia Tech. As the starting center, Tim was in the game from the very first moment, and all his fears faded away once the ball was in action.

Shot after shot sailed into the basket during a thrilling first half, with Tim making twelve of his sixteen attempts from the field. He was just as awesome on defense, racking up fifteen rebounds and shaming Georgia Tech, who managed a team total of only seven rebounds in the period. By the time Tim sank onto the bench to rest up during halftime, the Demon Deacons had a comfortable fifteen-point lead.

But any smart player knows that comfortable leads can be deceiving, and Georgia Tech fought back in the second half, soon going neck and neck with Wake Forest for the final crucial points. Georgia Tech's Stephon Marbury wouldn't give Tim a break. Every time the Deacons got off a shot, Marbury was right there to sink a matching one.

With eighteen seconds left in the game, Wake Forest held on to a slim 75–74 lead, but suddenly the ball was back in Marbury's hands. Tim was right on top of the talented player. "When I went to the basket and pulled up, Tim Duncan jumped," Marbury later described. "He pretty much overshadowed the basket."

Marbury missed his shot, and seconds later it was official. The Wake Forest Demon Deacons were ACC champs for the second year in a row! Grinning from ear to ear, Tim happily accepted the award for Most Valuable Player (MVP) of the game, which honored his game total of twenty-seven points and twenty-two rebounds.

Tim could hardly believe how far he'd come since the days when he hadn't even planned to play basketball. . . .

Chapter | One

A Rough Start

Tim's mother, Ione Duncan, was a midwife on St. Croix, one of the U.S. Virgin Islands, and she'd been present for the first breaths of many babies. Giving birth to her own children was still a very different experience, however, and Ione and her husband, William Duncan, were overjoyed at the birth of their third child—and first son—Timothy Theodore Duncan on April 25, 1976.

The baby of the family, Tim was adored by his parents and by his two older sisters, Cheryl and Tricia. He looked up to his sisters and as a young toddler began to follow in their footsteps in the sport that seemed to be an official family activity—swimming.

Swimming was more than a hobby for the Duncan girls. Both Cheryl and Tricia swam competitively, and as a teenager, Tricia became one of the strongest swimmers in St. Croix, even earning a spot as a backstroker on the 1988 U.S. Virgin Islands

Olympic squad. (The U.S. Virgin Islands are a commonwealth of the United States. Residents of the islands are considered U.S. citizens, but the islands function independently in many ways, including having their own Olympic team.)

Don't bother asking Tim how he liked third grade. Tim was so smart that he skipped directly from second grade to fourth at the age of eight.

Tim was bursting with pride in his sister, and he couldn't wait for his chance to compete for his homeland. By the time he was thirteen, he had set records in St. Croix for both the fifty-meter and one-hundred-meter freestyle. Everyone was convinced that Tim would be on the 1992 Olympic team. "Timmy was even better than me," raved Tricia. Ione was so devoted to supporting her children that she took night shifts at her job so that she'd be able to cheer on the kids at every swim meet. "She was my biggest fan," Tim says. "Every meet, she was the loudest parent there. Somehow I could always pick out her voice yelling over everybody else."

However, life took an unexpected turn, and the Duncan family suffered two tragedies in quick succession. Over the summer of 1989, Ione Duncan was diagnosed with breast cancer. She was undergoing treatment that September when Hurricane Hugo swept through the Caribbean region and devastated everything it touched. The Duncan family members were grateful to survive the storm that had killed dozens of people in the region and ruined thousands of homes on the island, but they still had to face the wreckage left behind. St. Croix had sustained a direct hit from Hugo, and the damage to properties across the island was extreme. Even the hospital where Ione was being treated faced problems, and her treatment had to be suspended while the facilities were repaired.

❝Swimming did a lot for me training-wise, because it's such an individual training situation where the workout is you get in the water and you do it. You have to find a way.**❞**

—TIM DUNCAN

Tim soon learned that Hugo had also destroyed the pool where his swim team practiced, along with other pools on St. Croix. The team's coach was forced to move practice to the ocean, which made Tim more than a little nervous. He had a terrible fear of sharks and decided to take some time off from swimming.

Tim believed he'd return to the sport, but more trouble lay ahead. Although Ione had resumed her treatments at the hospital, her illness still progressed. On April 24, 1990—just one day before Tim's fourteenth birthday—Ione died. With everything that had happened, swimming just didn't make sense for Tim anymore. "The hurricane broke Tim's routine by taking away our pool," Tricia explained. "Then when Mom passed, he lost his motivation." Swimming competitively had been so tied to his relationship with his mother, and it was hard for Tim to think about going to a meet without her.

The family underwent some changes to cope with their new situation. At the time of their mother's death, Cheryl Duncan had been living in Ohio with her husband, Ricky Lowery, and working as a nurse. She and Ricky moved to St. Croix to help William Duncan care for Tricia and Tim. The whole family did their best to support Tim. They understood why he no longer wanted to swim, but they also knew that he was a natural-born athlete. William couldn't help hoping his son would find another sport that he could enjoy—something to help him cope with his loss.

Cheryl agreed, and she had a certain sport in mind. One year earlier, Cheryl and Ricky had sent Tim a basketball hoop as a Christmas gift. When they arrived back on the island, they were surprised to discover that the basketball hoop had miraculously withstood Hurricane Hugo and was still firmly planted in the Duncans' backyard. Tim, a freshman at St. Dunstan's Episcopal High School, had joined his school's basketball team, but he wasn't exactly the team's star.

Try to guess the childhood nickname for this future NBA great, and you'll be stumped if you're thinking it had anything to do with Tim's basketball prowess. Nope, Tim was actually called "Mr. Clumsy" as a freshman, because he was so clumsy on the court!

Ricky, who had played college basketball in the United States, studied Tim closely and decided to start working out with him on that backyard hoop. Ricky was pretty sure he saw some raw potential in Tim. At age fourteen, Tim was already more than six feet tall. "He was uncoordinated," Ricky acknowledged. "But . . . when he saw a shot go up, he knew exactly where it was going to come down."

Ricky guessed Tim would grow to around six-foot five, so he decided to school his brother-in-law in the moves that mattered most for a player of that height. "We worked hard on his ballhandling skills because I thought he was going to be a guard," said Ricky. Basketball teams have two guard positions:

shooting guard and point guard. These positions go to the (relatively) smaller players, who are quick on their feet and able to move the ball down the court. Tim was a patient student, practicing intensively with Ricky and sometimes learning from just watching Ricky's moves.

All the hard work started to pay off in 1990, during Tim's sophomore year at St. Dunstan's, as he became more comfortable on the school's basketball squad. He also shot up, reaching six-foot five after one year and showing no signs of stopping there. Over the summer, Ricky brought Tim to Ohio to attend the Ohio State basketball camp, where Tim received more formal training in the sport. At the camp, Tim even had the chance to play against some college players. He managed to hold his own.

❝*[Ricky] was the one that taught me to handle and how to think the game and think about the game. He taught me a playground game.*❞

—TIM DUNCAN

By the time he returned to St. Dunstan's for his junior year, Tim had grown to nearly six-foot nine, and he was switched to center. The center position is played by the tallest member of the squad, and the role calls for strong defensive playing as well as scoring power close to the basket. Even though Tim's height meant he was tailor-made to play center, all of his previous training had taught him to take shots farther away from the basket. "I would shoot threes and drive and dish," Tim recalls. "I wasn't anything close to being a real center."

But as ever, Tim was willing to learn, and he soon adapted to his new place on the court. Once he began to master the skills he needed as a center, he became a pretty tough opponent to beat. He could actually combine the adept talent of a ball handler with his new size and strength. Look out, opposing teams!

Once Tim began to get psyched about basketball, he loved to watch his favorite player, Magic Johnson, in games on TV.

In fact, thanks to Tim, the St. Dunstan's squad quickly became one of the strongest teams on St. Croix. Unfortunately, being the best high school basketball player on a tiny island didn't mean a whole lot. In the United States, standout high school players quickly attract attention from college recruiters. But it was hard for college scouts to justify a long trip to the Virgin Islands, when there was a strong chance that a star player in the

Caribbean wouldn't be able to make it on their teams. A few recruiters came to check out Tim, but the scholarship offers coming in weren't what Ricky had expected for his brother-in-law. As graduation neared, Tim's future as a U.S. basketball star was looking uncertain—until one lucky break made all the difference.

Chapter | Two

Coming to America

One simple sentence began the next chapter of Tim's life. "Coach, there was a kid down there who played pretty well against Alonzo." The words were spoken by NBA rookie and former Wake Forest University student Chris King to his old Wake Forest coach, Dave Odom. "Alonzo" was Alonzo Mourning, the 1992 number-two NBA draft pick. "Down there" referred to St. Croix, where King had stopped earlier in the summer of 1992 along with other NBA rookies, playing in an international goodwill tour against local teams. Sponsored by the NBA, the tour gave new players a chance to sharpen their skills and to spread awareness and interest in American basketball outside the United States.

Coach Odom felt his heart start to race. A high school player who could guard NBA dynamo Alonzo Mourning? This was something he had to see for himself. Within days the coach had tracked down Tim's full name and address and his high school stats. Even though King hadn't known any of this information, he'd described Tim as being about six-ten. It wasn't hard to find a high school kid that tall who was known for basketball skills on St. Croix, where the island's total population at the time was somewhere around fifty thousand.

Tim met the Wake Forest coach at the airport and eagerly brought him to watch him play ball at his local outdoor court— one of just four on the entire island. The experience was completely different from what Coach Odom was used to back home, where a typical scouting trip meant checking out a high school game played in a gymnasium.

❝It's playground basketball [on St. Croix]. You have people of all ages playing against people of all ages.❞

—COACH ODOM

Still, Coach Odom did his best to judge Tim on his raw abilities, even though the game he was playing looked quite different from the play at Wake Forest. "As I watched him . . . I was impressed by his poise and composure and his presence on the court," Odom shared. "He was gangling and not an overly imposing player, but you could tell he had earned the respect of the older players out there."

By the end of the day, Coach Odom was sold. He came back to the Duncan household and sat down with Tim to watch a football game. During the game, Odom began his pitch, doing his best to convince Tim that he should come to Wake Forest. And that's how Coach Odom received his next piece of evidence that Tim was the right player for his team. As the coach gave his speech about the benefits of joining the Wake Forest program, he began to feel that Tim wasn't paying attention. Instead his eyes were glued to the TV screen. "The 49ers game was on," Tim explained. "And it was the fourth quarter."

Uh-oh, Coach Odom thought. Was he out here scouting a guy who wouldn't even listen to his own potential coach? Frustrated, he stopped talking and asked Tim if he'd heard a word he'd said. "He repeated back to me word for word what I had been telling him," Odom marvels. "I was amazed. He had this innate ability to look distracted, but still take in everything around him." The coach knew that ability would certainly come in handy in the middle of an action-packed college basketball game.

It turned out that Wake Forest wasn't the only school to express an interest in Tim. He was also recruited by the University of Hartford, the University of Delaware, and Providence College. For Tim, there was no question that he would accept an offer from one of the schools. Before his mother had passed away, she'd asked him to promise he would go to college and get a good education. It was a promise he took very seriously. In the end, Tim chose to go with Wake Forest, which offered him a full scholarship, along with the chance to learn from Coach Odom, who Tim liked a lot. Tim also had a good feeling about the college itself, which was in Winston-Salem, North Carolina.

Meanwhile Tim still had to finish his senior year of high school. He glided through his last basketball season at St. Dunstan's, averaging twenty-five points, twelve rebounds, and five blocks per game. Leaving his family and friends behind in St. Croix was tough for Tim, but he was excited to see what kind of future awaited him in the United States.

During college Tim began a tradition he has continued for the rest of his career—wearing his shorts backward in practice. He believes it brings him good luck!

Tim arrived at Wake Forest University in the fall of 1993, ready for anything and unsure what to expect. Having skipped a grade in elementary school, Tim was young—only seventeen. Coach Odom intended to hold Tim on the bench for a year to learn the game better. He planned to start him the following year at eighteen. This practice is called "redshirting," and the purpose is to have a player eligible for four full seasons of play. (The name comes from the red jersey that these players often wear in practices while playing with the regular team members.) Some students attend college for more than four years, but athletes can compete for only four seasons.

❝ *Once you see this kid play, you won't be talking about redshirting.* ❞

—WAKE FOREST UNIVERSITY SENIOR TRELONNIE OWENS

Coach Odom wanted to be certain that Tim was ready to bring his "playground game" to a Division I team playing in the ACC, the top conference in the National Collegiate Athletic Association (NCAA). Much attention was already being focused on some other ACC freshmen, like Jerry Stackhouse and Rasheed Wallace over at UNC in nearby Chapel Hill, North Carolina. Tim, on the other hand, was described by Street & Smith's college basketball annual as "pretty much of a mystery man."

Soon it became clear that the mystery was about to be solved one way or another. Odom's other first-year recruits, Makhtar Ndiaye from Senegal and Ricky Peral from Spain, were both forced to sit out the season for violating NCAA regulations. So the coach had no choice—he had to bring in Tim.

16

Tim found one supporter very early on. Randolph Childress—the star of the 1992–1993 Wake Forest Demon Deacons—liked what he saw the second he laid eyes on him. "One day I walk into the gym and see this tall guy who grabs a rebound, puts the ball between his legs, dribbles coast to coast, and slams," related Childress. He immediately ran to Coach Odom, who'd told him about a center from St. Croix who had lots of potential. "Hey, there's a tall kid in the gym doing incredible things," Childress raved to his coach. "If he's not Tim Duncan, you better recruit him—fast!"

❝He's got the best timing I've ever seen. He was blocking everybody's shots.❞
—TEAMMATE MARC BLUCAS, A SENIOR AT WAKE FOREST UNIVERSITY IN 1993

The enthusiasm from Childress encouraged Coach Odom to believe he'd made the right decision about Tim, but he knew the real answer would come on the court. In a very short time, Tim had moved from a likely status of being redshirted for the year to actually heading the team's starting lineup. The Deacons had another center, seven-foot-tall senior Stan King. But in practice Tim blew King away, establishing himself as the better player despite his inexperience. King graciously accepted that Tim should assume the starting role and even assisted in his training. "He's been a great teacher," Tim said at the time. "He overpowered me [in practice] and forced me to fight back because he knew how it was going to be in the league and I had no idea."

❝ *Tim Duncan was the best listener I ever coached. That mental approach combined with his physical skills is why he is such a great player.* ❞

—COACH ODOM

For all of Tim's skill and hard work, his first college game showcased the very problem Tim and his coach had worried about—his newness to this type of basketball. It was a road game against Alaska-Anchorage, a lower-ranked Division II team. Although the match should have been weighted in Wake Forest's favor, the Demon Deacons lost the game without a single point scored by Tim. In fact, Tim didn't even attempt a shot that game!

The loss was a deep disappointment, but Tim wasn't ready to give up that easily. He came roaring back in his team's next game, against Hawaii. Tim went from no points in his first game to an impressive double-double that night—double-digit numbers in both points and rebounds, with twelve in each category. It wasn't long before the Wake Forest "mystery man" was named ACC Rookie of the Week. And three weeks after that honor, he was named ACC *Player* of the Week!

The season continued to have ups and downs for Tim, but Coach Odom admired how well Tim handled the lows. Just as he'd rebounded so nicely from the first crushing loss, Tim could always take a bad game in stride. One night he faced Sharone Wright, a very tough center from Clemson. "Sharone handed Tim his head," Coach Odom says of that game. "It was a man against a young boy, one thunder dunk after another." The coach called Tim into his office the next day, prepared to give him a pep talk and help soothe over any mental wounds he assumed the freshman would be nursing. But midway into his speech, Tim interrupted and reassured Odom, "Coach, I'm fine. I'm just out there having a good time." Talk about a mature attitude!

During his freshman year, Tim set a Wake Forest record with 124 blocks.

By the end of the season, Tim was starting to get noticed. He finished the year with solid averages of 9.8 points and 9.6

rebounds per game. He could play through the pressure and had adapted to a different kind of basketball. He thrived on facing challenging opponents and took the rigorous schedule in stride. With Tim's help, the Demon Deacons—who'd rarely enjoyed a winning season in the past—ended up with a 20–11 record, good enough to qualify them for the NCAA Tournament. The NCAA Tournament takes place after each individual college-level conference tournament is completed, allowing teams throughout the entire NCAA to compete against one another to earn the title of the best college team in the entire country. The Deacons were eliminated from the tournament after two games, but Tim still had a lot to celebrate after a stunning first season.

The Goodwill Games were founded in 1986 by Ted Turner, who wanted to provide an opportunity for athletes from across the world to compete in friendly tournaments as a way to break down the walls between countries.

Tim couldn't wait to come back the following year and help his team make it even farther. In the meantime, his summer plans took shape when he received a last-minute invitation to join the

1994 USA Men's Goodwill Games Team in Moscow, Russia. The U.S. team was an elite squad made up of the top collegiate players in the country. Tim started in three of the five games for the American team, helping them win the bronze medal.

After the tournament, Tim toured Brazil for eight games with an ACC All-Star team led by Coach Odom. "Playing internationally has really helped my development," Tim said at the end of his summer abroad. "It gives me a chance to play against older, stronger, more experienced players."

Tim was quickly becoming one of those stronger, more experienced players himself. Suddenly everyone wanted to see what Tim would do next!

❝*He doesn't know how good he is yet.***❞**
—ESPN COMMENTATOR DICK VITALE ON TIM IN 1993

Chapter Three

Sophomore Superstar

The Wake Forest Demon Deacons had won the ACC league tournament just two times in the school's entire history. The most "recent" victory, in 1962, was a distant memory. In 1994, as Tim started his sophomore season alongside senior Randolph Childress, fans in Winston-Salem began to get excited that it just might be time for another run at that title.

First things first—the regular season. After a slow start, Tim was on fire. By the time he nabbed ACC Player of the Week in December, he was leading the league in rebounds, blocks, and shooting percentage.

Tim was certainly proving he could pull off feats that other Wake Forest players hadn't managed in years. In a game against Florida State in January 1995, he scored twenty-six points and grabbed twenty rebounds. It had been twenty-seven years since a Demon Deacon had nabbed a "twenty-twenty" like that. His twenty-three rebounds in a game against Winthrop was the highest anyone from his school had notched in thirty-three years.

Tim had strong support from his family during his college games, from near and far. His sister Tricia had moved to Baltimore, Maryland, working as a physical therapy aide. She attended as many of the Wake Forest games as she could and screamed her heart out for her little brother, reminding Tim of their mother at his swim meets. William Duncan was still in St. Croix, but his eyes were glued to the TV every time ESPN carried one of his son's games.

Tim had the mental toughness of a top athlete, too. Wake Forest had begun the season ranked fifth in the ACC, but Tim didn't let that affect his confidence. Against Duke University, an ACC powerhouse, Tim blocked seven shots, grabbed eight rebounds, and scored eighteen points to contribute to a 74–64 victory. He began to be known for having a poker face on the court—an unreadable expression that didn't show much emotion, intimidating opposing players. Tim was shaping up to be talented and smart, someone who used his brain as much as his body. "He always looks at tapes and studies the games," Coach

Odom said, praising Tim's efforts to learn from watching his own mistakes and studying other players' strengths and weaknesses.

Tim's stellar playing wasn't just about individual accomplishments, either. He and Childress worked hard to give their team win after win. By the end of the season Wake Forest had just five regular-season losses, the lowest in more than fifty years of the school's history. Tim was quick to credit Childress for helping him reach his new level of playing. "He pushed me," Tim said. "He demands the best from you, like he demands it of himself. . . . Now, I push along with him."

A lot had changed since Tim had arrived in North Carolina in 1993. His name was being said in the same sentences as the other top college players, and he no longer had the chance to patiently work on his skills in the shadows of the league's stars. But Coach Odom emphasized that the added pressure hadn't slowed down Tim one bit. Just the opposite, in fact. "The bigger the spotlight, the bigger the challenge, the better Tim seemed to play," Odom said.

As the 1993–1994 regular season wound to a close, Tim's skills were put to the ultimate test when Wake Forest traveled to the University of North Carolina's home court for one last matchup before the ACC tournament. Led by famous coach Dean Smith, the UNC Tar Heels were a major force in college basketball. They hadn't lost a home game all season, and the team was ranked second in the entire country. Fans geared up for an exciting rivalry between Tim and UNC sophomore Rasheed Wallace, expecting Wallace to put Tim in his place.

Twenty-five points and twelve rebounds later, Tim Duncan was having the last laugh. Suffocated by Tim's incredible defense, the Tar Heels' star was held to just four points. After Wake Forest finished with a 79–70 defeat of UNC—the first time they'd snagged a win in Chapel Hill in thirteen years—the spotlight on Tim was hotter than ever. Former NBA player Jerry West, then executive vice president of the Los Angeles Lakers, stated publicly that he believed Tim Duncan was the best player in the country. Talk about pressure!

❝*[Tim is] not flashy or spectacular, like Rasheed Wallace. But his game is so complete, he works so hard, and he just puts together great games on both ends of the floor.*❞

—CBS COMMENTATOR BILLY PACKER

After all the impressive performances during the regular season, the buzz around Winston-Salem reached a fever pitch as the Demon Deacons entered the 1995 ACC tournament. Would this be the year they'd finally come out on top?

It was the biggest question on Tim's mind but not the one he found himself answering from reporters. What *they* wanted to hear was whether Tim was going to enter that year's NBA draft. Other top college players—like Rasheed Wallace, Jerry Stackhouse, and Joe Smith—had hinted they'd be leaving college at the end of the year. Tim put the issue to rest almost as soon as it came up. "Man, the NBA is not even on my mind right now," he told the public. "I'm still enjoying the college life."

Tim kept such a calm and emotionless expression on his face during game time in college that some people called him "Spock," after the *Star Trek* character who never showed emotion. But Tim was known for being a real jokester off the court. He was always playing practical jokes on his friends—including picking their pockets when they weren't looking! Of course, he always returned whatever he took.

College life wasn't just about basketball for Tim. He had decided to major in psychology, and he really enjoyed his studies. "I love to think," he said. "I just love the inner workings of the mind." At that point, however, Tim focused on only one goal—helping his team win an ACC title.

The first battle in the tournament pitted Wake Forest against Duke, and the Deacons came away with a resounding 87–70 victory. Next up was Virginia, and Tim had extra motivation to play his best that night because his father was in the stands. It was the first college game William had watched his son play in person, and Tim didn't disappoint. He scored twenty points and drew repeated fouls from key Virginia players. Drawing fouls is helpful because after committing a certain number of fouls, a player is ejected from the game. In most of college basketball, the limit is five. (In certain situations the limit is six, as it is in the NBA.) But after players commit several fouls, coaches will rest them on the bench to protect them from being forced out of the game for good. So the more fouls Tim drew, the more time Virginia's best players had to spend on the bench, allowing the Demon Deacons to walk away with a final victory of 77–68.

The Demon Deacons had blazed a path to the ACC championship game. They were just one win away from the title, but it would be the toughest game of their season. To become the 1995 ACC champs, Wake Forest had to take down the UNC Tar Heels once again. They'd done it two weeks earlier in the regular season, but this was a do-or-die match, which was exactly when the Tar Heels were at their best. UNC had more ACC titles under its belt than any team in league history. After the recent loss to the Deacons, UNC was out for revenge—and redemption.

UNC came on strong, intimidating the Deacons in the first half and taking a 38–33 lead. Tim picked up three quick fouls, and Coach Odom warned him to pace himself and stay cool. Tim took a deep breath and focused on the game, avoiding adding any more fouls as the action continued. Still, with just under eight minutes on the clock, he couldn't help worrying, with his team down 61–55. When he found himself fighting Rasheed Wallace for another rebound, he used all of his strength and concentration to gain control of the ball without committing another foul.

Suddenly Wallace was on the floor, clutching his ankle. The injury took him out of the game, but no foul was called on Tim. With Wallace out, Wake Forest had a chance to rally. But Wallace's teammates struggled to hold on, and when the final buzzer sounded, the game was tied at seventy-three points apiece. The championship was going to be decided in overtime.

In the next five minutes of play, Randolph Childress reminded fans that he was the true leader of that year's Wake Forest squad, scoring all nine of his team's overtime points, including the final shot, with just 4.6 seconds left. That last basket gave the Demon Deacons an 82–80 win and their first ACC title in thirty-three years. Childress was the team's hero, but everyone knew he hadn't done it alone. Tim's sixteen points and twenty rebounds had been huge factors in the win.

In the final ten games of the 1994–1995 season, including the ACC tournament, Tim averaged an amazing 19.4 points and 13.3 rebounds per game.

Next up was the NCAA tournament. Wake Forest began by picking up two victories against lower-ranked teams. The Deacons came up against a tough team from Oklahoma State in the regional semifinals and lost 71–66, despite Tim's hefty contributions on scoring (twelve points) and defense (eight blocks and a whopping twenty-two rebounds).

Tim's sophomore basketball season had ended, but the honors were just beginning to roll in—National Defensive Player of the Year, All-ACC First Team, ACC All-Tournament team. Tim was red hot.

So red hot, in fact, that many questioned his decision not to enter the NBA draft—especially when the other sophomore phenoms opted to leave college early and go pro. UNC's Rasheed Wallace went to the team known at the time as the Washington Bullets (they later changed their name to the Washington Wizards). Maryland's Joe Smith was chosen as the first pick by the Golden State Warriors. The Warriors' general manager at the time, Dave Twardzik, admitted openly that it would have been Tim if he'd been available. "He's the best in college—it's not even close," Twardzik said of Tim.

"I was not ready," Tim said simply in response to those who wondered about his choice. "I just felt I was too young to be in the NBA." Also, Tim had promised his mother he'd finish college. He even took summer school classes to make up for classes he'd missed during basketball season. He loved the sport and saw his future out there on the court, but he wasn't about to give up on his education.

So while fellow sophomore stars like Joe Smith and Rasheed Wallace prepared to begin their rookie seasons with the NBA, Tim instead got revved up for his junior year at Wake Forest. As impressive as his performance with the Demon Deacons had been so far, he knew the next year would be crucial. Randolph Childress had graduated and entered the NBA, playing for the Portland Trail Blazers. It was time for Tim to take over as leader of his college team.

Chapter Four

Number One

Tim Duncan was ready. He'd worked hard over the summer to perfect his hook and jump shots, even though centers usually stick to dunks from right under the net. He'd also topped out at seven feet tall.

The Demon Deacons were psyched to learn that their first game of the 1995–1996 season would be against Oklahoma State—the team that had knocked them out of the previous year's NCAA tournament. A chance for revenge!

Tim wasn't about to let that chance slip away, and he turned in twenty-two points and grabbed seventeen rebounds to make sure his team got the victory. Nine of his baskets came straight in a row after Oklahoma reached within six points of the Deacons. In the end, the Deacons pulled off a huge win, 69–53.

It was a great way to start the season, but some bumps lay ahead for Tim. The first came in a match against University of

Massachusetts, led by junior center Marcus Camby, who was receiving a lot of attention after showing serious improvement that year. Before the game, an NBA scout released a statement comparing Camby to Tim, saying he believed "Camby has put himself in a position to challenge Duncan for the number one pick [in the NBA draft]."

The pressure got to both players, and neither was at his best in the December 6 matchup. Camby had more points in the game—seventeen to Tim's nine—but Tim grabbed twelve rebounds while Camby had nine. Tim also blocked four shots, one more than Camby. Still, Camby's Massachusetts squad won the all-important victory, taking the game by a whopping 60–46.

Tim did his best not to let the loss get him down, focusing on doing better next time. Too bad for the University of Florida at Gainesville, which faced the Demon Deacons three days later. Tim was everywhere on the court, finding his way around the massive defense assigned to him and helping Wake Forest to a 77–53 slaughter.

Fans of opposing teams gave Tim a hard time throughout the season. Playing against Duke's Blue Devils in their stadium, Tim had to listen to chants of "Camby, Camby," reminding him that he'd been the loser in that battle. In response, Tim scored twelve of the Deacons' final sixteen points in the last minutes of the game, beating Duke 57–54. During an away game at

Maryland, the insult screamed at Tim was "overrated." Oh yeah? Thirty-three points later—the most he'd ever scored in a college game—the yells died down. Maybe the fans were just distracted by watching their team lose, 85–78.

The season wasn't always easy for Tim, but he consistently fought back from every defeat with a stunning victory. By the time the 1996 ACC tournament got started, hopes were high for a repeat title for Wake Forest. They beat their first opponent, Virginia. Next was Clemson, which had taken Tim down during one of his low points of the regular season. Showing his usual ability to turn around a loss, Tim helped the Deacons derail Clemson with twenty-two points and a season-high nineteen rebounds.

Bart Bellairs, coach of the Virginia Military Institute basketball team, had a nightmare about taking on Tim Duncan right before his team had a game against the Demon Deacons. "What a horrible nightmare," Bellairs said. "Duncan wouldn't let me anywhere near the basket, and that night he wouldn't let any of my players near the basket, either."

The Deacons had done it—the team had made it back to the ACC championship game, with Tim heading up the squad. Its next and final opponent was Georgia Tech, the top performer in the ACC that season. Wake Forest was the defending champion but also the underdog in a fight against a team as skilled as Georgia Tech. With the roar of the crowd filling his ears, Tim charged ahead and made the basketball court his own. Fighting until the last seconds of the game, he helped Wake Forest grab their second straight ACC championship, 75–74. It didn't take long for Tim to win MVP of the game, as well as the entire tournament. He was also named ACC Player of the Year and elected to the NCAA All-America First Team.

Among his many nicknames, college teammates called Tim "Mr. Double-Double," for his amazing record of eighty-six double-double games out of the 128 he played in, and "Mr. Block," since he had at least one blocked shot in every single college game except for one.

Tim was thrilled to have another ACC title but longed for an NCAA one to match. Unfortunately, he came down with the flu just as the NCAA tournament began. His team rallied around him, and Wake Forest pulled off victories in the first two rounds against Northeast Louisiana and Texas.

The next round was against a tough Louisville team, and Tim psyched himself up to face them in his best, healthiest shape. He looked great in the first half, scoring eleven of the Deacons' first twenty points. But after getting into foul trouble—a fourth foul was called on him with about eight minutes remaining in the game—Tim wavered, and Louisville took a 59–54 lead. Realizing the game was slipping away, Tim and his teammates fought back, scoring baskets and making crucial foul shots. Their dedication paid off in the end. Tim's game total of twenty-seven points was a huge help in giving Wake Forest the tight 60–59 win.

Tim also blocked seven shots in the game against Louisville, breaking the record for blocked shots in an NCAA tournament. Interestingly, the record he broke had belonged to Alonzo Mourning, the very superstar who—indirectly—had helped Tim get to Wake Forest in the first place!

Tim had finally made it to the "Elite Eight" in the NCAA tournament, a semifinal round involving the eight top college teams in the entire country. Was this it—the year he'd make it all the way to the NCAA championship?

Wake Forest played Kentucky in the next round, and Tim knew the chances were slim. Kentucky had crushed its first three opponents in the tournament by margins of 38, 24, and 31 points. Sadly, the Deacons weren't able to change the story, losing to Kentucky 83–63. Still, Tim had helped his team make it farther in the tournament than Wake Forest had been since 1962.

Once again the question began to circulate—everyone wondered if Tim would skip his senior year and enter the 1996

NBA draft. Players as talented as Tim almost never stayed through four years of college. The risk of injury was too high, and many found the temptation of a multimillion-dollar salary too much to resist.

Tim had a total of four "twenty-twenty" games at Wake Forest, breaking twenty in points and rebounds.

The day before the deadline to apply for the draft, Tim waited in Coach Odom's office for a phone call from his coach, who was out of town. When the call came, Odom instructed Tim to turn over the two pieces of paper waiting on his desk. One was a letter to David Stern, the commissioner of the NBA, applying for the draft. The other letter was written to the sports information director at Wake Forest, giving him permission to hold a news conference announcing that Tim would be staying for his senior year of college. Coach Odom told Tim that the choice was entirely his, but he had to make it right then.

"I'm not going anywhere and I don't want a press conference," Tim replied. Coach Odom let out a major gasp of relief, but Tim didn't know why his coach had been so worried. He had made it clear that he intended to finish college and get a degree before moving on to the NBA, and that wasn't up for debate. His reasons were the same they'd been all along. He still felt too young, he wanted to complete his education, and—of course—he didn't want to break the promise he'd made to his mother.

---

66 *[Hearing that Tim had decided to stay at Wake Forest for his senior year] was a great relief, like hearing that somebody you love had made it through surgery. It's like the whole team was pacing nervously in the waiting room.* 99

—TEAMMATE SEAN ALLEN

On reflection, Tim's conviction made sense to Coach Odom. "His father and mother were both very committed to education," Odom shared. "But I think even more than that, they were committed to being yourself, taking your time, and not rushing nature—I think that was in him before he got to Wake Forest."

Tim may have been patient, but he was still every bit as hungry for the win. The Demon Deacons charged into the 1996–1997 season with a thirteen-game winning streak that brought Wake Forest to number two in the national rankings. Their ninth victory came over Utah, when Tim faced off with another great center and future NBA star, Keith Van Horn. This time Tim was the clear victor of the battle, helping his team to the final score of 70–59. It was obvious to everyone watching that Tim was getting better all the time, and Tim knew he'd made the right decision to stay and finish college. "I got stronger, smarter, and better prepared," he said.

Wake Forest's winning streak ended when Maryland managed a 54–51 defeat with a last-second three-point basket, but Tim's personal achievements throughout the season kept piling up. For the fourth consecutive year, he led the ACC in blocked shots. For the first time, he also led the whole nation in rebounding, averaging 14.7 rebounds per game. February 25, 1997, was the last home game of Tim's college basketball career. Playing Georgia Tech seemed like a perfect good-bye, but beating them was even better. Final score: Wake Forest, 71, Georgia Tech, 55.

❝*Someday your six-year-old kid will ask you for a Tim Duncan jersey for Christmas. This is your chance to play a future NBA Hall of Famer, your turn to face the greatest player any of you will ever meet.*❞

—WOFFORD COLLEGE COACH RICHARD JOHNSON TO HIS
PLAYERS BEFORE A 1997 GAME AGAINST WAKE FOREST

After the game, the school held a special ceremony to retire Tim's number 21 jersey. The stands were packed with fourteen thousand fans, but the ones who mattered most to Tim were his family, all beaming with pride. Randolph Childress also returned for the event, and even the governor of the U.S. Virgin Islands flew in for the occasion! The spectacle was overwhelming for Tim, who admitted to his audience, "This is probably the first time in my life that I'm uncomfortable on the court."

Unfortunately, Wake Forest wasn't able to repeat with one last ACC championship win for Tim, nor were they able to snag the NCAA title Tim had longed for so badly. No one blamed Tim for the losses, however. The sports world was too busy crowning him with practically every honor and award available to a college basketball player. Tim was once again named National Defensive Player of the Year and ACC Player of the Year and received multiple National Player of the Year awards, including the Naismith, given to the top college basketball player in the NCAA.

Coach Odom tried his best to wish Tim well without feeling too sad about losing him from his team. "Tim leaves us after four years of absolutely great performances," he said. "One monster game after another. I'm sad to see him go, but it's his time, and he's earned it."

Tim played in more winning games at Wake Forest University (ninety-seven) than any other player in the school's history.

Tim would, at last, be entering the NBA draft. He'd finished college and received his degree. He'd matured as a player, something even Michael "Air" Jordan himself commented on. "He's blossomed," Jordan said. "He stayed those four years in college and that dividend is starting to show." There was also no question that Tim would be the top draft pick. "I haven't seen a player in years who can do all the things [Tim] can," wrote NBA scout Marty Blake in his glowing report of Tim.

That left just one important issue unresolved. Which team would win first choice in the 1997 NBA draft lottery?

Chapter Five

Texas Titans

Every spring, an NBA draft lottery is held for all of the teams that failed to make that season's play-offs—the teams with the worst records of the year. The lottery is weighted so that the worst teams have the best chance at getting the highest draft picks. Picture a bowl with lots of names inside, and imagine that the worse a team's record is, the more slips of paper with their name on it are in the bowl, so the higher the chance that their name will be chosen. The draft lottery allows the worst teams to improve because they are able to choose from among the best new players entering the NBA.

As much as a team wants to win while the season's in action, once it's out of the running for the play-offs, having the absolute worst record becomes a good thing. Of course, losing the most games in a season may give a team the best shot at receiving the top draft pick, but it doesn't guarantee this will happen since it's still a lottery. This way teams can't try to lose games on purpose knowing they will definitely get a high draft pick. Their chances in the lottery will be better, but there will be other teams who could also snatch that high pick away if luck is with them.

In 1997 the Boston Celtics "won" the title of top losers, with the worst record in the league. The Celtics were competing against twelve other teams in the lottery, but the team was hopeful about grabbing the top pick and adding Tim Duncan to their roster.

Tim watched the televised lottery from his childhood home in St. Croix, anxious to see where his new home would be. He could barely contain his excitement as NBA commissioner David Stern began to announce the draft picks in reverse order. When Stern was down to the final three teams, Tim's ears perked up. This was it—he was about to learn which team he'd be playing for!

To many people's surprise, the team with the third pick turned out to be . . . the Boston Celtics. "I sat up in my chair when Boston came up early," Tim said later. He'd been as sure as everyone else that he was likely to end up a Celtic. But it was down to San Antonio and Philadelphia. "I was an excited, nervous wreck at this point," San Antonio Spurs chairman Peter Holt said.

Holt didn't have to be nervous for long. Seconds later David Stern announced that Philadelphia had the number-two choice, giving San Antonio the number one draft pick. Miles away in St. Croix, Tim felt like *he* had just won the lottery. The San Antonio Spurs had been a very strong team throughout the decade, led by All-Star and 1995 MVP David Robinson. During the 1996–1997 season, Robinson had been on the bench because of problems with his back and foot. Joining him for parts of the season were teammates Chuck Person, Charles Smith, and Sean Elliott. Missing these standout players, the Spurs had won only twenty games that year, a shocking drop from their usual strong records.

The lottery is based solely on the previous season, without considering the reasons for a team's performance, their performance in past seasons, or their ability to perform in the next season even without a top draft pick. Most teams with poor records would continue to struggle without that new player. This wasn't the case for the Spurs, however, since Robinson and Elliott were both recovering and would be ready to play again in the 1997–1998 season. Tim wasn't starting his NBA career on a team where he'd immediately have to carry all the weight. Instead he was giving an already talented team one more giant boost. Some players might have felt a little disappointed that they wouldn't be the only star of the team, but Tim couldn't have been happier at how it all turned out. "I think I was really blessed," he admitted. "We have an opportunity to win a lot of games our first year and that's different from most number one picks who have to go in and rebuild a team."

❝I don't mind getting the fourth pick. What I mind is having to face Robinson and Duncan in the West four times a year. That's the real kicker.❞

—Stu Jackson, president and general manager of the Vancouver Grizzlies, after the 1997 NBA draft lottery

---

The Spurs' coach, Greg Popovich, also felt blessed to have such a deeply talented squad to work with. He did have one problem, though. What would he do with two great big men, Tim and David Robinson? They were both excellent players, and he wanted to use them together somehow, but they played the same position—center. Only one center could be on the court at a time.

The solution came from something that Tim's brother-in-law Ricky had set in motion many years earlier, when he'd underestimated how tall Tim would be. Ricky had taught Tim the necessary skills to play an "outside" game, meaning that Tim could play well from areas of the court that are outside the area just under the basket, the domain of the center. It's uncommon for a center to be so versatile, and Tim's huge range of abilities was part of why he'd excelled in college. Those abilities also allowed Coach Popovich to use Tim as either a center or a power forward so that Tim and the equally flexible Robinson could play side by side. "[Tim] can shoot the jumper. He's got range to the three point line," Popovich raved. "He's got jump hooks right and left. He can catch it, pull it through, and drive on people."

The "problem" of having two great centers seemed to be solved. Still, other teams had tried to make things work with two big men in the past, and the combination often failed to produce good results. Too much of a good thing? It really was possible because the players tended to get in each other's way at the basket. Sometimes their egos also got in the way. If each player was out to get the best stats on scoring and rebounds, then it was almost like the two teammates were competing against each other, not just the opposing team.

David Robinson was used to being the only center for the San Antonio Spurs as well as the center of attention. In 1987 Robinson had been the Spurs' number one draft pick. Due to a two-year military service commitment, he didn't actually play for the team until the 1989–1990 season. Robinson, nicknamed "The Admiral," had wowed the world of college basketball with his amazing feats for his team at the U.S. Naval Academy. Like Tim, Robinson blasted through records and was named Player of the Year his senior year of college.

In 1989–1990, his rookie season with the Spurs, Robinson helped the team to the biggest single-season turnaround in the history of the NBA. San Antonio won a whopping thirty-five more games that year than they had the previous season. Their final regular-season record was 56–26, and the Spurs won their division title. Robinson continued to be the driving force as the Spurs grew stronger every year. In 1995 the team's 62–20 record was the best in the NBA's entire league, and Robinson was crowned MVP. San Antonio made it all the way to the Western Conference finals but lost out on the chance to advance to the NBA finals to the Houston Rockets.

So how would a player like David Robinson react to a newcomer who threatened to push him off his pedestal? Anyone who worried about the issue didn't know what kind of player—or person—David Robinson was. His first move was to invite Tim to his summer home in Aspen, Colorado. That way the two of them could train together and Robinson could start teaching Tim everything he would need to know to be prepared for the pros. What David really wanted wasn't to be a star himself but to play for a winning team. He knew if he and Tim could form a strong enough partnership on the court, they could make that happen. After a couple days of one-on-one in Aspen, things were looking good. "I worked him pretty hard," Robinson admitted, "and he never complained."

Luckily the two not only worked well together, they also quickly became friends. "He's the real thing," Robinson said of Tim. "A lot of guys come in and don't want to do anything, but he gives all that extra effort and work and is open to help and wants to become a better player."

In response, Tim said, "It's great to see David's training regimen, gain some of the knowledge he's acquired in the years he's been in the league. It helped me set goals and understand what it will take to succeed."

David did his best to help Tim feel prepared for the start of his first year in the NBA, but Tim couldn't help feeling scared when the time finally came. "I used to wake up at 4:00 AM going, 'Oh my God, am I good enough to play with these guys?'" Tim was the only one asking that question. Everyone else was too busy being amazed at the way Tim not only met their expectations but jumped right past them. In a preseason game against the Houston Rockets, Tim pulled one of his classic double-doubles with a matching seventeen points and seventeen rebounds. Impressed,

Rockets star Charles Barkley said, "I have seen the future and he wears number 21," referring to Tim's jersey number. Number 21 left his mark on the first official game of the regular season. The Spurs were playing the Denver Nuggets, and Tim scored fifteen points and grabbed ten rebounds to help his team win the game 107–96.

Meanwhile Robinson was better than ever with Tim at his side. "The better [Tim] is, the more my game is going to flow," he said. Coaches and players in the NBA began to refer to Tim and David as the "Twin Towers," realizing that this dynamic duo was unlike any that had come before. Combined, the two players averaged 42.1 points and 24.4 rebounds a game during the first thirty-two games of the season.

Tim became the second rookie ever to make the All-Star team when he was named to the squad for the February 1998 game. The first? David Robinson!

In a game against Michael Jordan's championship Chicago Bulls, Tim and David fought the champion team every step of the way, forcing the game into not one but *two* overtime periods before eventually losing by just four points. Tim matched Bulls top-notch defender Dennis Rodman rebound for rebound for a total of twenty-two, and whenever he wasn't there, David Robinson was. "We had to shoot jump shots," Jordan said after the game, explaining the challenge he and his teammates had faced. "And believe me, I tried to get to the basket. But with those Twin Towers sitting in the middle, it was tough."

Tim was already impressing Michael Jordan! Clearly there were some exciting days ahead with Tim and David Robinson together.

❞*You have to rethink the rules when you play those guys. You get by one of them, and the next thing you know you're facing his clone.*❞

—Houston Rockets coach Rudy Tomjanovich
on Tim and David

Chapter Six

On the Brink

There was no question that with Tim and David playing together, the Spurs were at the head of the pack. But if he needed to do it, could Tim still get the job done by himself? In February 1998, when David was forced to sit out six games with an inflamed knee, fans were about to find out.

Tim came through with flying colors. He made up for his missing teammate by boosting his regular averages to an even higher 25.3 points, 13 rebounds, and 4.5 blocked shots per game, helping the Spurs win four out of the six games.

As Tim continued to sail through his rookie season, he kept racking up Rookie of the Month awards. In fact, he won the honor for every single month of the entire basketball season. Only two other players had ever done that before. Houston Rockets center Ralph Sampson had been the first, in the 1983–1984 season. The next had been a player whose footsteps

Tim seemed to be following in more ways than he could count—David Robinson.

Tim and David had so much in common, it almost seemed like fate had brought them together. As if there weren't enough parallels, the San Antonio Spurs' 1997–1998 regular-season record of 56–26—thirty-six more wins than in the previous season—added another to the list. David Robinson had led the Spurs to the biggest turnaround ever eight years earlier, in his rookie year. Rookie Tim Duncan, fresh out of college, had helped David and the rest of the Spurs break their own record!

❝Tim has an incredibly quick mind. You show him something once and you'll never have to show him again.**❞**

—DAVID ROBINSON

Tim's next challenge was bringing the Spurs to the NBA championship. San Antonio's strong season had earned them a spot in the 1998 play-off tournament, and they faced the Phoenix Suns in the first round. The NBA play-off tournaments consist of three rounds—first round, conference semifinals, and conference finals. Until recently, the first round was a best-of-five series, so that whichever team won three out of five games advanced to the next level. The semifinals and finals were both best-of-seven series (and remain so today), with teams needing to win four out of seven games to advance. The top eight teams from the Eastern Conference play one another in these play-offs, while the top eight teams in the Western Conference do the same. The winning Eastern Conference team then plays the winning Western Conference team in the NBA finals.

Game one of the first round of the 1998 play-offs belonged to Tim, who scored an unbelievable thirty-two points in his first-ever NBA postseason game, along with pulling down ten rebounds. The Spurs won, 102–96. Danny Ainge, coach of the Suns, was shocked, especially by the fact that twenty-eight of Tim's points came in the second half. "For a rookie in his first play-off game, in the fourth quarter—in clutch time!—he was as good as some of the best players who have ever played," Ainge marveled. "I guess I underestimated Tim Duncan."

Ainge wasn't going to make the same mistake twice. He instructed his players to swarm Tim on defense in the second game, and the efforts paid off with a 108–101 defeat of the Spurs.

The night of the third game in the series, Tim was announced as the NBA Rookie of the Year after receiving 113 out of 116 possible votes. Tim was thrilled to receive the award but quick to credit his teammates for the roles they had played. "I was fortunate because I didn't have to come in and save the team," he said. "There were . . . great players who were already here. All I had to do was fit in and learn my way."

Inspired by his award, Tim came back with a vengeance in the next two games. After a victory in game three, San Antonio was just one win away from advancing to the next round of the conference play-offs. Tim poured in twenty-two points and fourteen rebounds to make it happen in game four, which the Spurs won 100–88.

Next up was the Utah Jazz in the Western Conference semifinals, featuring star player Karl Malone. Tim was everywhere during the first game of the series, trying to stop the Jazz, who kept racking up points during the first three quarters. He even outscored the entire Jazz squad 17–15 in the fourth quarter, giving everything he had to help his team come out on top. Unfortunately, all his hard work was lost when he missed a jump shot in the final moments that would have prevented Utah from their slim 83–82 victory.

Utah rode the momentum to win the second game 109–106 in overtime. The Spurs held on with an 86–84 triumph in game three, but the Jazz took the next two games of the best-of-seven matchup and won the series, 4–1.

Tim was the first rookie since Larry Bird back in 1980 to make the All-NBA First Team.

Tim's first NBA season was over. The twenty-two-year-old hadn't brought his team to the finals, but he *had* helped them complete an amazing leap from the previous year. He'd also enjoyed other aspects of playing professional basketball. For instance, he discovered an interest in traveling. "Every time I went on a road trip," he said, "there was another new place that I hadn't seen before, another situation I'd never been in, and new players I'd never seen." Another benefit of being an NBA star for Tim was the opportunity his salary and growing fame gave him to help people and causes that mattered to him. As soon as he joined the Spurs, he became an active participant with the Spurs Foundation, which helps organizations like the United Way and the Children's Bereavement Center of South Texas. Tim had a special place in his heart for other children who suffered the loss of a parent, as he had, and wanted to do what he could to help those children.

Meanwhile Tim had amazingly established himself among the top players in the league in just his very first season in the NBA. And he was already thinking of ways to improve for next year. Unfortunately, "next year" didn't start when it usually did. The 1998–1999 season was delayed by a contract dispute between owners and players that pushed the opening game from the fall all the way into February 1999. Instead of the regular eighty-two games, time allowed for only a fifty-game season.

Tim and his teammates were excited to return to the court, but getting their bodies back into shape took a little more time. Suddenly they had to readjust to a rigorous schedule of games after being away from their jobs for many months. Tim showed his usual dedication, making the team his first priority. He had an extra motivation to play his hardest since once negotiations between the owners and the Players Association were finally completed, Michael Jordan had announced his retirement. With Jordan, the Chicago Bulls had dominated the NBA for most of the decade. Jordan's retirement created an opening for another team—led by a new standout player—to take over the throne.

❝ *There's a maturity about him in understanding that he can be the heir apparent in this league. He understands the responsibility and work ethic that entails.* ❞
—SPURS COACH GREG POPOVICH

As the shortened 1998–1999 season began, that team seemed unlikely to be the Spurs. February was a rough month, and the Spurs lost eight out of their first fourteen games. Then on March 2, the Spurs scored a victory over the Houston Rockets that became the first of a nine-game winning streak. San Antonio breezed through the rest of the season, adding just five losses and finishing with a tie for the best record in the league, 37–13. Karl Malone's Utah Jazz also had a 37–13 record, but the Spurs came out on top since they'd beaten the Jazz two games to one during their regular-season series. Malone was still named league MVP, but Tim didn't mind. He'd rather see his team come out ahead. "The thing about Tim is that he is not playing for MVP awards," his teammate and friend Antonio Daniels said. "He's playing for championships."

Speaking of championships . . . it was time for the 1999 play-offs! The Spurs' first-round opponents were the Minnesota Timberwolves. The Wolves squeezed just one win into the mix before being knocked out. Next came the Los Angeles Lakers. Tim knew he faced a challenge in Lakers center Shaquille O'Neal, one of the best big men in the league. Fans wondered if O'Neal and his talented teammates, including phenomenal guard Kobe Bryant and forward Robert Horry, had what it took to knock out Tim and the Spurs.

Not this time, they didn't. San Antonio swept the Lakers in four quick games. Tim started off strong in game one and sank a game-winning jump shot in game two. If that wasn't enough to rile up the Lakers fans, game three was the Tim Duncan show. He scored an incredible thirty-seven points—matching the team's wins in the regular season. Even more impressively, nineteen of Tim's points came from free throws at the foul line. Teams often use a strategy of fouling the opposing center when it looks like the center is about to make a basket because traditionally centers have more trouble than other players making foul shots. Foul shots were widely known as the one major flaw in Shaquille O'Neal's game. O'Neal's struggles at the foul line made life easier for the Spurs during their play-off series, but it wouldn't have helped much if the Spurs' big men, David and Tim, had the same problem. Tim's ability to shoot from a distance came in handy once again. After losing the series, Lakers power forward Robert Horry said, "[Tim's] got a lot of weapons. Too many."

Tim was the only NBA player to rank in the top ten in the league for scoring (sixth), rebounding (fifth), blocked shots (seventh), and field goal percentage (tenth) in the 1998–1999 season.

Thanks to Tim's arsenal of basketball weapons, the Spurs advanced to the Western Conference championship. They had already made it farther than they had in 1998, but Tim wouldn't be happy until he had that NBA finals ring. To get there, he had to bring his team a Western Conference title first, and the Portland Trail Blazers stood in the way. That wasn't a problem for Tim, especially since he didn't have to face his old college teammate Randolph Childress, who had been traded from the team. Four wins later—including one by an astounding forty-four-point-margin victory—the Spurs had trampled over the Trail Blazers. As always, Tim had shone in the postseason, averaging 23.2 points and 11.5 rebounds in the play-offs. More important for Tim was that his team was headed to the finals.

The New York Knicks took the Eastern Conference title, and they were just as hungry to go all the way as the Spurs. But the Knicks were at a disadvantage because their star center, Patrick Ewing, was on the bench with an injury. Even so, the team's supporting players had all stepped up in Ewing's absence. Latrell Sprewell, who had just joined the Knicks that season, was a serious threat. He was known for making seemingly impossible baskets, and he was lightning fast on the court. The Knicks, like the Spurs, were a strong defensive team, which made for an interesting matchup with the Spurs.

During the shortened 1998–1999 season, Tim matched his team's record of thirty-seven wins with thirty-seven of his trademark double-doubles, leading the league in this category for the second year in a row.

Duncan at Wake Forest—signaling for a pass

"Slam Duncan" slams one during a 2002 game against the Philadelphia 76ers.

Duncan grabs a loose ball in front of Shaquille O'Neal during game four of the 2003 Western Conference semifinals.

Tim Duncan's commitment to charity includes his spending time with members of the Boys & Girls Clubs of San Antonio.

Duncan's fans display their support for the two-time MVP.

Duncan shows off his goofy side during a break in the action in game four of the 2003 Western Conference semifinals against the Los Angeles Lakers.

Duncan shows great consistency in his free throws—something that sets him apart from many of the other centers in the NBA.

Dribbling down the court for Team USA during a 2003 Olympic qualifying match against Puerto Rico

Duncan and David Robinson hold their trophies high as they celebrate their victory at the 2003 NBA Finals.

The San Antonio stadium was packed with 175 of Tim's friends for the first game of the 1999 finals. Tim was determined to put on a good show for them. He scored thirty-three points with his usual impressive variety of shots and grabbed sixteen rebounds. The final score was 89–77, Spurs.

❝[Tim] gave the league a breathtaking look at its future.❞

—SPORTSWRITER MIKE WISE

The Spurs followed this great start with another easy victory, 80–67. As some experts had predicted, the overall scoring in the series wasn't very high since both teams were loaded with skilled defensive players. To win a game in the 1999 finals, a team had to find a way to get through the other team's defense. So far the Spurs had been cornering that market, but in game three the Knicks found their rhythm. Despite twenty points from Tim, the Spurs fell to the Knicks, 89–81.

Summoning an extra reserve of energy, the Spurs came back in game four with everything they had. Impressively, every single starting player on the San Antonio squad scored in the double digits, with Tim contributing twenty-eight points. The result was a 96–69 blowout for the Spurs, putting them within reach of an NBA championship. Just one more win and the trophy would be theirs.

Tim knew how much everyone was counting on him—his coach, his teammates, and most of all his best friend and partner, David Robinson. Robinson had achieved a great deal in his decade in the NBA, but he had never taken home an NBA title. Tim hoped with all his heart that he could help make that happen.

Chapter Seven

Slam Duncan

Game five of the 1999 NBA finals took place in New York City's Madison Square Garden. This wasn't just any old stadium. Located in the heart of New York City, Madison Square Garden is the most famous basketball home court in the country. At the time, the Garden boasted a long-standing record of sellout crowds. New York fans who crammed into the stands were passionate supporters of their Knicks, prepared to make every Spurs basket as tough as it could be.

❝Basketball is like a chess game; you cannot reveal all that you are thinking or you will be at a sizable disadvantage to your opponent.❞

—TIM DUNCAN

The Knicks weren't about to let those fans down. As the game got going, Latrell Sprewell, who came from the Golden State Warriors, showed everyone why the Knicks management had brought him on board. He helped New York jump to an early lead of 21–15. Tim fought back, bringing the Spurs to within one point of the Knicks by the start of the second quarter. His body was charged with nervous energy. "Tim . . . doesn't show his emotions too much, but he was hyped up for game five," David Robinson said. The excitement was a little much for Tim, and he sat down for a short break to rest. As soon as Tim landed on the bench, the Knicks went wild. New York led by eight points when Tim returned to the court, and he knew he had to get serious.

Sprewell was just as determined, and as the fans watched, the game became a duel between the two players. Tim and Sprewell continued to trade baskets, each more impressive than the last. As different as their skills were, the players shared the same fire to win and an ability to come up with new tricks at every turn.

With slightly more than three minutes remaining in the game, the Knicks had a two-point edge, 77–75. Sprewell took a shot to bring the lead to four but missed. Tim, however, made a foul shot and cut the margin down to one point. The seconds ticked away as each team struggled to find an in. The Knicks were clinging to their slim lead and the chance to come back in the finals series. The Spurs wanted to end it right there. Under a minute left, and the pressure was beyond intense. Who would make the next move, Tim or Latrell?

Actually, it was neither. Spurs point guard Avery Johnson cut through the tension with a perfect two-pointer, putting San Antonio ahead by one. It was all on Sprewell to pull another quick move and win things for New York. With 2.1 seconds left, Sprewell looked, dodged around the Spurs defenders to catch a pass, and then headed straight for the basket. Fans held their breath. They knew Sprewell could be unstoppable when he was truly on fire.

At least, unstoppable by the average NBA defender. When Tim and David Robinson raced to set up their infamous "Twin Towers" block, Sprewell faltered and missed his shot. The buzzer sounded, and San Antonio had their victory, 78–77. They had clinched the team's first NBA title in its twenty-six-year history.

Tim's playing in the finals series had been extraordinary, and it was downright unbelievable since he had just turned twenty-three and was only in his second year in the league.

---

66 *Tim doesn't play like a second-year player. When you see a seven-footer hitting twenty-foot bank shots, the guy's a special talent.* 99

—New York Knicks coach Jeff Van Gundy

It was no surprise when Tim was crowned MVP of the finals after averaging 27.4 points and 14 rebounds a game. David Robinson was 100 percent behind him. "It's . . . a great feeling having Tim Duncan by my side," Robinson later said in an interview with *Sports Illustrated*. "He's obviously the best player in the league. Tim was phenomenal against New York, and his finals MVP award was well deserved."

Tim, David, and their teammates congratulated one another with big hugs. In the midst of it all, Tim pulled out a small video camera and taped his friends so he could preserve the thrill forever.

After the trophies were presented, a reporter asked Tim what he would do next to commemorate the triumph. "I have no idea," he said. "I'll just celebrate as much as possible until I have to be in training camp in a few weeks."

That was the Tim Duncan those closest to him knew. Even right after such a huge accomplishment, Tim's focus was already turning to his next task. He had been asked to play with the USA Basketball Men's Senior National Team, often called Team USA, in the 1999 summer international qualifying matches. A strong showing in the matches would secure the team's spot in the 2000 Olympics. Many countries send teams to the qualifying tournament, held the year before the Olympics, and only the top teams from that round go on to actually compete at the Olympics.

Before Team USA's training camp, however, Tim had to finish up that celebrating he'd mentioned. Back home in San Antonio, Texas, the fans were ready and waiting to shower their team with gratitude for bringing thcm an NBA title. Thousands of people waited at the airport to greet the returning heroes. An even more massive crowd of 250,000 fans showed up for the official victory parade down San Antonio's Riverwalk. The Spurs rode down the river in specially made boats, waving to everyone and showing off their long-awaited trophy.

After all of the celebrating, it was time to get back to work. NBA coach Larry Brown, then coach of the Philadelphia 76ers, was in charge of Team USA, and he was immediately impressed with Tim. When Brown arrived at the first qualifying game two hours early, he saw a few players already practicing. He scanned the room, assuming the superstar members of the team wouldn't be there until close to the start of the game. No, wait—was that Tim Duncan out there? Of course it was. Tim didn't listen when everyone said he didn't have to worry about these games since the Americans were heavily favored to win. He was a member of a team, which meant he would arrive early and practice hard to play his best.

As predicted, the U.S. team cruised through their matches, easily securing a place in the 2000 Olympic Games. Tim couldn't wait to represent his country. In the meantime, he was psyched to rejoin the Spurs and attempt to win another NBA title.

In September 1999, before the new basketball season began, the Spurs were invited to one more celebration of their championship win. This one took place at the home of someone who claimed to be a huge basketball fan. He was also the president of the United States. Tim was headed to the White House! Tim had a great time visiting President Bill Clinton but was reminded that all eyes would be on him to help San Antonio stay on top for the 1999–2000 season.

During the Spurs' visit to the White House in 1999, President Clinton told Tim he hoped he could imitate Tim's "killer look" when he faced budget negotiations with Congress that fall, referring to the emotionless poker face that Tim had been known for since college.

As the season got started, Coach Popovich came to Tim with a special request. Sean Elliott, who played the small forward position for the Spurs, was going to have to miss the season due to a kidney illness. Popovich had been trying to figure out the smartest way to fix the hole in their starting lineup. The team was strong on tall players, so he felt he could afford to move Tim into Elliott's position for short periods during the games, with someone else filling in for Tim at power forward or center. It's very unusual to play someone who would normally be a center or power forward as small forward, a position that calls for more speed and the ability to take shots farther from the basket. Yet Tim was such a strong all-around player that he was able to excel in the role. "Tim's at another level," his teammate Mario Elle said in awe.

Another level, all right. Even with the changes he had to make in his game that season, Tim averaged 23.2 points and 12.4 rebounds. He was thrilled to have another chance to play in the All-Star game, which hadn't been held the previous year due to the shortened season. Making up for lost time, Tim poured in twenty-four points and grabbed fourteen rebounds. He was named co-MVP of the game, sharing the honor with fellow big man Shaquille O'Neal.

Tim and David's "Twin Towers" defense was as strong as ever in 1999–2000. The Spurs had the record for least amount of points allowed by their opposing teams, an average of 90.2 points per game.

In February 2000, following the All-Star break, Tim strained a stomach muscle that kept him on the bench for four games. He was eager to get back into the action but unfortunately suffered a second injury in April, tearing cartilage in his left knee. He missed another four games—the last four of the regular season. Worse, he was forced to sit out the entire play-offs. "I know he's dying to play," David Robinson said. "But if you can't run, you can't play. It's just that simple."

What wasn't simple for Tim was watching his team play—and lose—without being able to help them out. The Spurs fell to the Phoenix Suns in the first round of the play-offs, three games to one. (Once a team has won the three games it takes to win the series, no further games are necessary.) The disappointment didn't end there. After having surgery on his knee in May, Tim also missed competing with the U.S. team at the 2000 Olympics, where they won the gold medal. Tim just hoped he'd be in better health when the next Olympics rolled around in 2004.

Back in San Antonio, Tim had a decision to make as he recuperated from his knee surgery. He had become a free agent, meaning that he could sign with any team in the NBA. The Orlando Magic, the Chicago Bulls, and the New York Knicks were among the teams expressing interest. Fans in San Antonio kept their fingers crossed and let out a giant sigh of relief in July when Tim announced he was staying put. "When it came down to it, I liked what I had here," he said.

Looking ahead, Tim stayed focused on his future with the Spurs. "I know I have a lot of work to do and a long way to go," he said modestly. Tim was never afraid of hard work. He was up for whatever came next as long as it brought his team closer to another championship win!

Chapter Eight

Most Valuable Person

Tim was in tip-top shape and raring to go as the 2000–2001 season began. He was back in the game in a big way, averaging 22.2 points, 12.2 rebounds, and three assists per game. For the third year in a row, Tim made the All-NBA First Team along with the NBA All-Defensive First Team. These are dream "teams" made up of the five strongest players in the entire league in certain categories, voted on by writers and broadcasters from the sports media world. The very best defensive players, for instance, are voted onto the All-Defensive First Team. The All-NBA First Team is the best of the best—players who are most outstanding in their all-around game.

With Tim leading the charge, the Spurs zoomed through the season and finished with the best record in the league, fifty-eight wins and twenty-four losses. Would this be the year they'd reclaim their championship title? It sure looked promising.

Tim was only the second player in NBA history to be named to the All-NBA First Team and All-Defensive Team in each of his first three seasons in the league. The first? Guess who—David Robinson!

San Antonio faced the Minnesota Timberwolves in the first round, just as they had in their successful bid for the championship in 1999. History repeated itself as the Spurs came away with a series victory after four games, winning three games to the Wolves' one. Tim knocked down five points in the last two and a half minutes of game four to secure a solid lead and to win the game and the series.

Next up was a new play-off challenger for San Antonio, the Dallas Mavericks. The Dallas squad had come a long way that season, and the Mavs were eager to finish strong. They showed their inexperience at the play-off level—their last play-off appearance had been in 1990—in the first three games of the series, however, losing each by significant margins. It looked like the series was in the bag for the Spurs, but Dallas finally fought back in game four. The Mavericks rallied for a 112–108 victory, and Tim realized he couldn't let them open that door any farther. He poured in thirty-two points and pulled down a monstrous twenty rebounds in game five to help San Antonio crush the Mavericks, 105–87.

---

66 Mom never got to see Timmy play ball seriously. But I think she's looking down from heaven cheering him on—the loudest voice among all the angels. 99
—CHERYL DUNCAN LOWERY

The Spurs had made it back to the Western Conference finals. This time they faced the Los Angeles Lakers, the team they had swept in the 1999 play-offs. But the 2001 Lakers were a very different team than they had been two years earlier. Under coach Phil Jackson—who had brought Michael Jordan's Chicago Bulls six NBA championships—the Lakers had assumed the NBA throne in 2000.

The Lakers were out to repeat, and they were looking good in game one, which Los Angeles won 104–90. Tim did his best to block the Lakers in game two. He scored twenty-five points in the first half alone and finished with a career play-off high of forty points—in essence half of his entire team's total of eighty-one. But Tim couldn't do it alone, and the Lakers still managed to win.

Games three and four were disastrous for the Spurs. Tim admitted having an off night in game three, scoring only nine points as the Lakers steamrolled over the Spurs 111–72. The series was wrapped up in the next game, 111–82. Nothing was stopping those Lakers, not even Tim Duncan.

Sadly, the season was over for the Spurs. But Tim had plenty of exciting developments in his life off the court to distract him from the disappointing loss. Most exciting was his wedding to longtime girlfriend Amy Sherrill, a fellow Wake Forest University graduate, in the summer of 2001.

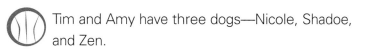 Tim and Amy have three dogs—Nicole, Shadoe, and Zen.

Amy shared Tim's dedication to helping people, and together the couple formed the Tim Duncan Foundation, set up to serve "the areas of education, youth sports and recreation, and health awareness and research." The foundation focuses on causes that benefit cancer research as well as community needs in San Antonio, Winston-Salem, North Carolina (where Tim went to college), and the U.S. Virgin Islands.

Tim had remained involved with charity work since he began during his rookie season, but the foundation he and his wife created allowed him to attract even more public focus and funding to the causes he believed in so strongly. Along with its fund-raising efforts throughout the year, every January the Tim Duncan Foundation holds the Bowling for Dollar$ Charity Bowl-A-Thon to raise money for breast and prostate cancer detection, prevention, and research.

In 2001 Tim was honored with the Home Team Community Service Award by the NBA and the Fannie Mae Foundation, recognizing his help in rebuilding inner-city neighborhoods. The award offered Tim the opportunity to choose two charities to receive $25,000 donations each in his name. Tim chose the San Antonio Children's Shelter—the largest and oldest shelter for abused, abandoned, and neglected children in Bexar County—for one award and gave the other half of the money to social service organizations in the Virgin Islands.

Tim is clearly as serious about helping people in need as he is about scoring wins on the basketball court. But it's not all serious business with Tim. His teammates admire his ability to relax and have fun. "He busts into my room on road trips and, if there's a basketball game on, he makes me turn to wrestling," says Tim's teammate and friend Antonio Daniels. "We're in each other's rooms hours a day, watching TV and laughing."

 Tim has a huge collection of knives, including a real three-foot-long Japanese samurai sword!

Apart from basketball, Tim's biggest passion is video games. He has so much game equipment at home, he can't even fit it all into one room. Tim loves to challenge his teammates to play against him. Former teammate Sean Elliott had considered himself the video game king until he played Tim. "You have to understand, I don't lose at home," Elliott said. But when he invited Tim over, it was a different story. "He made me go out and buy a game manual so I can study the moves more," Elliott recounted.

Tim is also famous for his pranks. Once he told Spurs coach Greg Popovich that they needed to talk about ace teammate Avery Johnson, the Spurs' starting point guard. Keeping a straight face, Tim told Popovich that he should be playing point guard instead of Johnson. "C'mon, Coach," Tim said to Popovich. "We all know that Avery Johnson is not that good!" Tim knew full well that Johnson was within earshot when he made the comment, and soon all three of them had cracked up laughing.

That was the Tim his friends and teammates were used to, but reporters and fans had started to think Tim didn't have a friendly, funny side because they only saw his intensity during basketball games. Tim decided to share the quirkier parts of his personality with the public and wrote an article called "What Lurks Behind That Smirk: The Psychoanalysis of Tim Duncan" for *Sport Magazine.* In the article, Tim explained that he thought it was important to keep a poker face while he was playing so that the other team couldn't guess his emotions and use that to its advantage. However, he admitted to being a silly guy who liked to have fun with people. He even jokingly suggested having his own line of clothing, like other famous athletes, except that his clothes would all involve some sort of surprise. As examples, he mentioned a pair of pants on which one leg would be longer than the other or an item of clothing that would turn a different color after being washed.

Tim has several tattoos, including one of the wizard Merlin from the legend of King Arthur.

It was no longer a secret that Tim could be a pretty goofy guy. His charity work and marriage to Amy were also public knowledge, giving Tim a solid reputation for being an all-around kind and loyal person. What amazed fans was that Tim could be all of those things and still hadn't lost an ounce of his fierceness or his competitive drive.

As excited as Tim was about being married and launching the Tim Duncan Foundation, he was just as eager to sink his teeth into another season with the Spurs. It had been too long since he'd played in the NBA finals. Tim was more than ready to bring the Spurs another championship title. He knew that meant taking his already incredible skills up another notch.

Chapter | Nine

Fast Break

Going into the 2001–2002 season, many thought Tim Duncan couldn't get any better. He'd already taken the league by storm, he'd won an NBA title, he'd been named co-MVP of an All-Star game, and he'd brought home stats that would make Magic Johnson himself proud.

But Tim didn't see it that way. New accomplishments still awaited. While having an NBA MVP award was never a priority over helping the Spurs win as a team, Tim still hoped that he could bring his playing to the level where he could earn the biggest compliment in professional basketball.

Some athletes become distracted when their personal lives are full. Tim had a new bride to focus on and a new foundation to oversee. Along with all of the happy distractions was a sad one. Tim's father was ill, and Tim worried about his condition. But despite all of these things, Tim stunned the basketball world by managing to improve on what was already an amazing career. His numbers on offense and defense were mind-blowing, including a career-high fifty-three points in a December game against the Dallas Mavericks.

❝*Some things come easy to me.*❞

—TIM DUNCAN

The Spurs finished the season with another strong 58–24 record, and they were back in the play-offs. Would they make it to the finals this time?

San Antonio was up against the Seattle Sonics in the first round of the play-offs. Tim knew he had an extra-tough job ahead because David Robinson was suffering from a lower back sprain that kept him out of the action. Still, the Spurs were able to trounce the Sonics in game one, 110–89. Seattle showed its teeth in the second game, pulling ahead for a 98–90 victory. Oh yeah? The Spurs came right back to show who was boss with another decisive defeat of Seattle in game three, 102–75.

The thrills and pressures of the basketball season were interrupted by a personal tragedy. William Duncan faced a sudden crisis with his illness and passed away without much warning. Tim was devastated to lose his second parent, especially since the

Duncan family had always remained very close. William's funeral was scheduled to take place in the Virgin Islands, and Tim needed to be there. He traveled first to North Carolina, where his father had been living, and then to his old home in St. Croix to be a part of the service. As a result, Tim missed the fourth game of the play-off series against Seattle. Some fans accused Tim of deserting them at a critical point in the season, especially with David Robinson injured. Seattle won game four, 91–79, pushing the series to a deciding game five. Although the Spurs were disappointed, neither Coach Popovich nor any of Tim's teammates questioned Tim's decision. In their minds, as in Tim's, it wasn't even a decision. Family came first, definitely before basketball.

The loss of his father was deeply painful for Tim, but when the funeral was over, he returned to play in the fifth and final game of the Seattle series. Basketball was his dream job and helped him escape all of his grief. "When [Tim] steps on the court, he concentrates on basketball," said Coach Popovich. "Nothing throws him off, he's a stoic character, but I bet he knows what he's feeling."

Popovich had faith in Tim's ability to play through his pain, and Tim came through in game five. He knocked down twenty-three points and racked up nine rebounds and seven blocks. His efforts paid off in a satisfying victory for the Spurs, 101–78, advancing them to the next round of the 2002 play-offs. "It's been a whirlwind," Tim admitted after the game. "It's been a tough couple of days. That's an understatement. [But] I've had great support from my family and friends."

Tim's emotional roller coaster wasn't over because after the round against the Sonics, it was time for the season's MVP honor to be announced. Tim's name was being mentioned as a top contender, but other star players had also made huge contributions to their teams that year, like center Shaquille O'Neal for the Lakers and the Nets' dynamo point guard Jason Kidd.

These guys did great work, and so did many other top NBA players. But when the 2002 NBA MVP was announced, Tim's coach and teammates were thrilled to hear he'd won! Tim was overwhelmed by the moment. He'd made it all the way to the top of the league, and at the young age of twenty-six, his massive efforts for the Spurs were being recognized in a major way.

Along with being voted the NBA MVP in 2002, Tim won the IBM Award, a computerized calculation of which player in the league makes the strongest contributions to his team.

Next the Spurs once again had to play the Los Angeles Lakers in a crucial best-of-seven play-off series. This time it was the Western Conference semifinals, and the Lakers, who had won the championship title for the past two years, were psyched to go for a third championship. Their star center, Shaquille O'Neal, was also ready to prove he was the better big man.

The series didn't start well for the Spurs, who lost to Los Angeles 86–80. Tim wasn't about to see his team go through another Lakers sweep, and he helped tie the series with an 88–85 victory in the second game. The Lakers pulled out ahead again in game three, 99–89. Game four was close, but the final score of 87–85 gave Los Angeles a two-point win. The clincher was game five. If San Antonio lost, it was out of the play-offs and its 2002 season would be over.

Tim did everything he could to avoid a loss for his team. Still dealing with the raw emotions from his father's death, Tim went to work on the court and scored thirty-four points. He even grabbed a franchise play-off record twenty-five rebounds, dazzling fans with his staggering defense. Sadly, Tim's heroics weren't enough. The Lakers walked away with a 93–87 triumph and eventually won their third straight championship with a sweep of the Eastern Conference champs, the New Jersey Nets.

During the off-season, Tim spent quality time with his wife and family, treasuring the moments with loved ones more than ever. He rested his body and spirit and prepared to return to the league in the 2002–2003 season. This year he was determined to bring that championship trophy back home to Texas.

Tim's teammates on the Spurs were just as determined, and together they finished the season with a strong 60–22 record. Tim was the clear leader of the squad, and the team expected that he would bring home a second straight MVP award. All he wanted, though, was to show the fans that he could be a true MVP and bring the San Antonio Spurs another championship. The mission had even more urgency because David Robinson had announced he planned to retire at the end of the season. Tim had so much respect and admiration for Robinson, and he wanted to give his teammate a proper good-bye.

❝*[Tim is] a quiet assassin who is skilled in all aspects of the game.*❞

—NBA COACH GEORGE KARL

The Spurs' first-round opponents were the Phoenix Suns. This year, however, it would take more than three wins out of five to advance to the next round. Beginning in the 2003 play-offs, the NBA had extended the first round of play-offs from five games to seven. That meant the players would need more stamina than they were used to at that point in the play-offs in order to win four out of the seven games. It also meant the Spurs didn't have to worry as much when they lost the first game, 96–95, after a tight overtime contest.

Still, there was no room for complacency. San Antonio evened the score with a win in game two, then added another victory in game three. The Suns came back in game four but lost to the Spurs in game five. Tim sealed the deal in the sixth game, ensuring that the Spurs had a spot in the Western Conference semifinals.

Unfortunately, San Antonio faced a familiar enemy in the semifinals—the Los Angeles Lakers. The Lakers had edged them out over and over again. Would they do it once more in 2003? Not if Tim had anything to say about it.

Tim's confidence got a major boost before the series began when, as predicted, he was named NBA MVP for the second consecutive season. Led by their MVP, the Spurs charged ahead, winning the first two games of the series and giving the Lakers a good scare. Los Angeles rallied, taking back games three and four. Tim sank twenty-seven points and grabbed fourteen rebounds in game five, helping the Spurs take a 3–2 lead in the series. It was time for game six, the deciding game if San Antonio could win it since it would give them the necessary four victories to advance.

The answer came in the form of a whopping thirty-seven points and sixteen rebounds from Tim, during a game in which the Spurs never trailed after the very first minute of action. The three-time NBA champion Lakers lost their spirit as the Spurs knocked down basket after basket, bringing the final score to an embarrassing 110–82 slam fest. No one had been able to stop Los Angeles for three years, but in 2003 the Lakers were starting their vacations a lot earlier than they were used to.

❝A steady diet of Tim Duncan was the recipe the San Antonio Spurs used to end the reign of the Los Angeles Lakers.**❞**

—NBA.COM SPORTSWRITER

Of course, the battle to the finals wasn't over yet. The Dallas Mavericks still stood in the way, offering Texans an all-Texas matchup that really got the fans going. The Mavericks made it clear in game one of the Western Conference finals that they wouldn't go down easy, winning 113–110. The Spurs sent the message right back in game two, with a 119–106 defeat of the Mavs. "Duncan was huge," said Dallas player Dirk Nowitzki after the game. "Every time we really got close, he picked up a huge rebound or a huge basket that would put the momentum back in their favor."

Nowitzki and his fellow Mavericks went all out in the next game to stop Tim from another one-man takeover. Their efforts failed, however, when Nowitzki suffered a knee injury while fighting for a rebound. He was forced to watch from the bench while the Spurs beat his team, 96–83, and then added another win in game four.

Heading into game five, the Spurs prepared to finish the job. Nowitzki was still out of commission, and the win seemed like a sure thing. By early in the third quarter, the Spurs had a 66–49 lead. But Dallas wasn't ready to give up just yet. The Mavericks struggled back for a 103–91 victory, pushing the series to at least one more game.

The pressure had never been this intense. The Spurs were just one win away from returning to the NBA finals—one win away from Tim's dream of sharing another championship with David Robinson. It was time to find out if that dream had a chance to come true.

Chapter Ten

A Perfect Moment

Game six of the 2003 Western Conference finals took place in the Dallas Mavericks' stadium. Luckily San Antonio was used to winning crucial games on the road. Could they do it this time, with everything on the line?

The Mavs were just as desperate for a win—more desperate, in fact, since a loss in that game would eliminate them from the series. They showed how much a victory meant to them by playing hard through the third quarter, running up a fifteen-point lead over the Spurs. San Antonio was looking weak, and game seven seemed around the corner.

Slowly but surely, the Spurs began to catch up. Early in the fourth quarter, Tim sank a foul shot, and the basket seemed to light a fire under his teammates. Suddenly the San Antonio squad was red hot. The Spurs racked up an amazing twenty-three straight points without allowing a single basket from the

Mavericks. Finally Dallas snuck a few in, but in the end San Antonio outscored them 34–9 in the quarter—enough to lock in the lead and the game, 90–78.

The Spurs were going back to the NBA finals!

Tim was so ecstatic, he could barely contain his excitement. He knew that this was meant to be. All he needed was to do it again in four more games, and he'd be able to send David Robinson into retirement in style. That meant the New Jersey Nets, the Eastern Conference champions, would have to get ready for a major battle if they thought they were going home with the NBA title.

The 2003 NBA finals was the first time two teams formerly from the American Basketball Association (ABA) league had played against each other in the NBA championship. The ABA was an alternative basketball league existing along with the NBA in the 1960s and 1970s. When the ABA folded, four of its teams were brought into the NBA—the Nets, the Spurs, the Indiana Pacers, and the Denver Nuggets.

The Nets were indeed up for a good fight at their second straight appearance in the finals. They'd been swept by the Lakers in 2002, and they weren't about to get trounced like that again. But Tim Duncan made it his personal mission to keep the Nets from getting what they wanted. Once Tim found his rhythm against New Jersey in game one, he was unstoppable, scoring twenty-four of his thirty-two points in the second half of the game. He also added twenty rebounds, seven blocks, and six assists. The Spurs took down the Nets 101–89. Ouch.

Byron Scott, coach of the New Jersey Nets, realized he needed to rethink his strategy fast. In game two, he had his players double and triple teaming Tim, doing whatever they could to shut him down. Nets center Dikembe Mutombo—a four-time Defensive Player of the Year—turned up the heat, limiting Tim to just nineteen points. Even so, the Spurs stayed neck and neck with the Nets into the final moments of the game. But when the final buzzer sounded, the Nets had the edge, leaving the court with an 87–85 victory.

The series was tied one game apiece, and the Spurs didn't like that one bit. Tim was thrilled to see the way his teammates came together to help him out in game three. Huge contributions came from Spurs point guard Tony Parker and guard Manu Ginobili. The Nets realized that even all their hard work to stop Tim wasn't going to cut it because he had a cast of supporting players who could come through as well. While Parker, Ginobili, and the rest of the San Antonio squad did their part, Tim continued to play his usual smart and steady game, even while being smothered by the New Jersey defense. "[Tim] is an amazing player, because it doesn't matter what gets taken away from him," raved Coach Popovich. "He finds another way to be involved, whether it's getting rebounds, assists, blocked shots— he's really an all-around player." Playing as a team, the Spurs beat the Nets 84–79.

Game four was an off night for both the Nets and the Spurs, producing one of the lowest-scoring games in NBA finals history. New Jersey scored just eleven points total in the third quarter, tying a thirty-one-year record low set by the New York Knicks. Still, the Nets were able to get some momentum going in the final quarter, and they squeaked out a 77–76 defeat of the Spurs. Uh-oh.

The Nets had leveled the playing field again, even if they'd only barely managed the win. The outcome of the series was becoming more and more uncertain. The Spurs knew they had to come on strong in game five and set a new take-no-prisoners tone for the series. Tim did just that, of course. He had another monster game with twenty-nine points, seventeen rebounds, and four blocks. Meanwhile Steve Kerr, one of Tim's most experienced fellow Spurs, stole the spotlight briefly. He had made a famous clutch play on another championship team, the Chicago Bulls, back in the 1997 NBA finals. He'd played in the league for fifteen years and knew how to keep his cool. With the Spurs in foul trouble, Popovich sent out Kerr and watched as he scored six points in the final three minutes of the game, helping San Antonio move comfortably to a solid lead. The Spurs scored a decisive victory, 93–83.

It was time for another high-stakes game six. If the Spurs won this game, they'd be NBA champions again. San Antonio had a mental advantage going in three games to two. The Nets were fighting to stay alive, and the Spurs just wanted to close things up quickly. Overconfidence was still dangerous, however. If the team wanted to win the game, Tim had to be prepared for anything.

Tim knew how much winning game six mattered. He'd proved many times over what kind of a player he was, but in game six, his performance was downright awe inspiring. He came close to achieving a *quadruple*-double by nearly landing in the double digits for four different categories of stats. He nailed the triple-double for scoring, rebounds, and assists with totals of twenty-one, twenty, and ten, respectively. The narrow miss came in blocks—Tim had eight, which itself tied a finals record.

The dazzling Tim Duncan show wasn't just about numbers. Every move was unbelievable, every basket perfectly timed to boost the team when it needed it most. Seven of Tim's points came in the last five-and-a-half minutes of the second quarter, pulling the Spurs to a tie with New Jersey, which had shot ahead.

The Nets players gave it their best, but Tim refused to be denied. The game belonged to Tim from the moment it began. When it was over, the final score proved it—88–77, Spurs.

 Tim averaged 24.2 points, 17 rebounds, 5.3 assists, and a finals record 5.3 blocks in the 2003 NBA finals.

The San Antonio Spurs were the 2003 NBA champions. Tim was so overwhelmed, he could barely breathe. He ran to hug his wife while David Robinson celebrated with his family. Robinson had also enjoyed a stellar game, saying good-bye to the league with thirteen points and seventeen rebounds.

The triumph was a thousand times more meaningful than Tim and David's first NBA title, for so many reasons. This win came after a full-length regular season, unlike the one in 1999, meaning it would go down in the record books without an asterisk. Tim had shown the world he was a true MVP, bringing his team all the way for the second time in five years. The Spurs had grabbed victory on their home court, surrounded by San Antonio fans cheering them on. "It's an incredible feeling to do it here . . . to give our fans a kind of a treat," Tim said after the game. Most of all, this championship was unforgettable because Tim and David had done it together, for the last time.

❝One of the biggest thrills [of the 2003 NBA finals] was playing those last final minutes with Big D [David Robinson]. To be able to send him off that way was huge for us and for him.**❞**

—TIM DUNCAN

Emotions were intense during the postgame awards ceremony, held right there on the court with confetti everywhere. NBA commissioner David Stern presented the Spurs with their championship award and handed Tim the MVP award for the series. Tim and David stood arm in arm, holding their trophies up in the air triumphantly. It was a precious moment, and Tim knew he would cherish the memory forever.

The celebrations didn't end there, and once again San Antonio went all out to show the Spurs its gratitude. Tim didn't have too long to revel in his latest victory, however. He still had a lot of work ahead of him.

First up were the qualifying matches with Team USA to secure the team's spot in the 2004 Olympics. Tim still wished he hadn't had to miss the 2000 tournament, and he was determined to make it there in 2004, especially since his own coach, Greg Popovich, was on board as an assistant coach for the national squad.

Tim joined an elite group of NBA stars training for the American team's summer matches. Last-minute injuries caused some changes in the planned lineup, but Tim remained front and center as Team USA began its first round in late August. America sailed through the competition, beating each opponent by a wide margin. With a 9–0 winning streak, Team USA faced off against Argentina for the gold medal final round of the tournament. They nailed a 106–73 victory, making the record a clean 10–0 and giving spectators a nice glimpse of what lay ahead in 2004.

There was no doubt about it—2003 had been a fantastic year for Tim. The best part is, he's still just at the beginning of a fabulous basketball career.

One of the Good Guys

Tim Duncan has received a long list of awards and honors over the course of his short basketball career. Most recognize his athletic accomplishments, and many acknowledge his devotion to charity work. Some might say that the award that speaks best about who Tim is as a player and a person is his nomination as one of the "Good Guys" in sports by *Sporting News.*

These "good guys" are athletes who demonstrate generosity of spirit on and off the court. They put their teams' success ahead of personal glory, and they go above and beyond to take care of their communities. A leader in this category, Tim has established himself as a true class act—a source of pride for the entire NBA.

In fact, Tim's many wonderful qualities were further recognized when *Sports Illustrated* announced their Sportsmen of the Year in December 2003. Tim and David graced the cover of the magazine's issue, sharing this one last honor together. "The remarkable combination of skill and sportsmanship that Tim and David displayed on the court is matched only by their sense of duty and commitment to their community," said Terry McDonell, managing editor of *Sports Illustrated.* "They are good neighbors and truly amazing athletes. It is that combination that makes them our Sportsmen of the Year."

❝*On behalf of the people in my hometown of San Antonio, I'd like to express how proud I am of the entire Spurs organization, especially David Robinson and Tim Duncan, and all that they have given to the community.*❞

—U.S. SENATOR AND SAN ANTONIO NATIVE JOHN CORNYN DURING A SPURS VISIT TO THE WHITE HOUSE IN OCTOBER 2003

As the 2003–2004 season got going, Tim was busy as both a neighbor and an athlete. While he rejoined the Spurs for another run at the championship, Tim's foundation was busy organizing more charity events to benefit the many worthwhile causes it funds. Tim's official Web site proudly shares that the foundation has raised more than $500,000 since its creation. Tim also uses the Web site to keep in touch with his fans through diary entries, showing his appreciation for their support.

Tim knew that support would be more important than ever as he faced a new challenge—his first season playing without David Robinson at his side. "We have a very different team this year and it's going to take some time for everyone to gel and learn the system," Tim wrote in an entry on his Web site in the fall. "With hard work and your support, I think we will come together very well."

After a rocky start, including a sprained ankle that kept Tim on the bench in early November, the Spurs began to gain momentum over the winter. With Tim at the helm, there's every reason to believe the San Antonio Spurs have many more exciting victories to look forward to in the future!

PERSONAL STATISTICS

Name:

Timothy Theodore Duncan

Nickname:

Slam Duncan

Born:

April 25, 1976

Height:

7'

Weight:

260 lbs.

Position:

Center/Forward

CAREER STATISTICS

Season	Team	Games	Rebounds	Assists	Steals	Blocks	Points	Season scoring average
1997–98	SAS	82	977	224	55	206	1,731	21.1
1998–99	SAS	50	571	121	45	126	1,084	21.7
1999–00	SAS	74	918	234	66	165	1,716	23.2
2000–01	SAS	82	997	245	70	192	1,820	22.2
2001–02	SAS	82	1,042	307	61	203	2,089	25.5
2002–03	SAS	81	1,043	316	55	237	1,884	23.3
2003–04*	SAS	49	629	159	49	132	1,130	22.9
TOTAL		500	6,177	1,606	401	1,261	11,454	22.9

*as of February 17, 2004

AWARDS

National Player of the Year (college), 1996–97 (AP, U.S. Basketball Writers, Naismith, Wooden, CBS/Chevrolet, NABC)

National Defensive Player of the Year (college), 1995, 1996, 1997

ACC Player of the Year, 1996, 1997

NBA Most Valuable Player, 2002, 2003

NBA finals MVP, 1999, 2003

IBM Award (all-around contributions to team's success), 2002

All-NBA First Team, 1998, 1999, 2000, 2001, 2002, 2003

NBA All-Defensive First Team, 1999, 2000, 2001, 2002, 2003

NBA All-Defensive Second Team, 1998

NBA Rookie of the Year, 1998

NBA All-Rookie First Team, 1998

NBA All-Star Game Co-MVP, 2000

NBA All-Star, 1998, 2000, 2001, 2002, 2003

SOURCES

3   Rappoport, Ken, *Tim Duncan: Star Forward,* (Berkeley Heights, NJ: Enslow Publishers, 2000), 69.

5   Stewart, Mark. *Tim Duncan: Tower of Power,* (Brookfield, CT: Millbrook Press, 1999), 5.

5   Rappoport, *Tim Duncan: Star Forward,* 18.

6   Torres, John Albert, *Sports Great Tim Duncan,* (Berkeley Heights, NJ: Enslow Publishers, 2000), 18.

7   Rappoport, *Tim Duncan: Star Forward,* 23–24.

8   Byman, Jeremy, *Great Athletes: Tim Duncan,* (Greensboro, NC: Morgan Reynolds, 2000), 15.

8   Rappoport, *Tim Duncan: Star Forward,* 29.

9   Ibid., 30.

10 Byman, *Great Athletes: Tim Duncan,* 16.

12 Rappoport, *Tim Duncan: Star Forward,* 34.

13 Ibid., 41.

13 Ibid., 36–37.

14 Byman, *Great Athletes: Tim Duncan,* 18.

14 Stewart, *Tim Duncan: Tower of Power,* 14–15.

16 Rappoport, *Tim Duncan: Star Forward,* 44.

16 Stewart, *Tim Duncan: Tower of Power,* 17.

17 Ibid., 16

17 Rappoport, *Tim Duncan: Star Forward,* 44.

18 Ibid., 45

18 Torres, *Sports Great Tim Duncan,* 28.

19 Rappoport, *Tim Duncan: Star Forward,* 46.

19 Ibid.

21 Torres, *Sports Great Tim Duncan,* 23.

21 Stewart, *Tim Duncan: Tower of Power,* 19.

23 Byman, *Great Athletes: Tim Duncan,* 26.

24 Ibid., 24–25.

26 Stewart, *Tim Duncan: Tower of Power,* 22.

25 Rappoport, *Tim Duncan: Star Forward,* 51.

26 Stewart, *Tim Duncan: Tower of Power,* 22.

26 Thornley, Stew, *Super Sports Star Tim Duncan,* (Berkeley Heights, NJ: Enslow Publishers, 2001), 21.

30 Stewart, *Tim Duncan: Tower of Power,* 25.

30 Ibid., 24.

32 Rappoport, *Tim Duncan: Star Forward,* 58.

33 Torres, *Sports Great Tim Duncan,* 30.

36 Rappoport, *Tim Duncan: Star Forward,* 77.

37 Stewart, *Tim Duncan: Tower of Power,* 29.

37 Ibid.

38 Torres, *Sports Great Tim Duncan,* 33.

38 Byman, *Great Athletes: Tim Duncan,* 41.

39 Rappoport, *Tim Duncan: Star Forward,* 82.

40 Byman, *Great Athletes: Tim Duncan,* 44.

40 Torres, *Sports Great Tim Duncan,* 35.

40 Ibid., 34.

42 Ibid., 37.

42 Rappoport, *Tim Duncan: Star Forward,* 87.

43–44 Torres, *Sports Great Tim Duncan,* 39.

44 Rappoport, *Tim Duncan: Star Forward,* 87.

45 Torres, *Sports Great Tim Duncan,* 40.

46 Stewart, *Tim Duncan: Tower of Power,* 38.

47 Ibid., 39.

47 Torres, *Sports Great Tim Duncan,* 40.

47 Ibid., 41.

47 Ibid., 43.

48 Byman, *Great Athletes: Tim Duncan,* 47.

48 Stewart, *Tim Duncan: Tower of Power*, 39.

49 Rappoport, *Tim Duncan: Star Forward*, 91.

49 Taylor, Phil, "Two for the Show," *Sports Illustrated*, November 24, 1997, 58

51 Rappoport, *Tim Duncan: Star Forward*, 11.

52 Stewart, *Tim Duncan: Tower of Power*, 44.

52 Torres, *Sports Great Tim Duncan*, 49.

54 Stewart, *Tim Duncan: Tower of Power*, 43–44.

55 Torres, *Sports Great Tim Duncan*, 53.

56 Ibid., 55.

57 Ibid., 11.

59 Ibid., 45.

61 Byman, *Great Athletes: Tim Duncan*, 53.

62 Torres, *Sports Great Tim Duncan*, 9.

63 Byman, *Great Athletes: Tim Duncan*, 11.

64 Knotts, Bob, *Sports Superstars: 8 of Today's Hottest Athletes*, (New York: Rosen Publishing Group, 2003), 59.

64 Torres, *Sports Great Tim Duncan*, 13.

66 Byman, *Great Athletes: Tim Duncan*, 56.

67 Torres, *Sports Great Tim Duncan*, 56.

68 Knotts, *Sports Superstars: 8 of Today's Hottest Athletes*, 60.

69 Ibid.

69 Torres, *Sports Great Tim Duncan*, 60.

72 Stewart, *Tim Duncan: Tower of Power*, 27.

73 SlamDuncan.com

74 Knotts, *Sports Superstars: 8 of Today's Hottest Athletes*, 56.

75 Ibid.

75 Torres, *Sports Great Tim Duncan*, 44.

79 Stewart, *Tim Duncan: Tower of Power*, 11.

80 "With Heavy Hearts, Spurs Do Their Part," *NBA.com*, May 3, 2002, <http://www.nba.com/games /20020503/SEASAS/recap.html> (January 27, 2004).

80–81 Ibid.

83 Stewart, *Tim Duncan: Tower of Power*, 21.

85 "Spurs, Tim, Dunk Lakers, Head to Conference Finals," *NBA.com*, May 15, 2003, <http://www.nba.com /games/20030515/SASLAL/recap .html> (January 27, 2004).

85 "Spurs Tie Mavs as Series Shifts to Dallas," *NBA.com*, May 21, 2003, <http://www.nba.com/games /20030521/DALSAS/recap.html> (January 27, 2004).

90 "Spurs Take Game 3, Home Court From Nets," *NBA.com*, June 8, 2003, <http://www.nba.com/games /20030608/SASNJN/recap.html> (January 27, 2004).

92 "Spurs Cut Down Nets to Win NBA Title," *NBA.com*, June 15, 2003, <www.nba.com/games/20030615 /NJNSAS/recap.html> (January 27, 2004).

93 Duncan, Tim, "NBA Champions," *SlamDuncan.com*, n.d., <http ://www.slamduncan.com/diary -champions.php> (January 28, 2004).

96 "Tim Duncan and David Robinson Named Sports Illustrated's 2003 Sportsmen of the Year," *SlamDuncan.com*, n.d., <http ://www.slamduncan.com /news-si.php> (January 28, 2004).

96 "President Bush Honors Tim & Spurs," *SlamDuncan.com*, n.d., <http://www.slamduncan.com /news-whitehouse.php> (January 28, 2004)/

97 "The New Season" *SlamDuncan .com*, n.d., <http://www .slamduncan.com/diary- newseason.php> (January 28, 2004).

BIBLIOGRAPHY

Byman, Jeremy. *Great Athletes: Tim Duncan.* Greensboro, NC: Morgan Reynolds, 2000.

Knotts, Bob. *Sports Superstars: 8 of Today's Hottest Athletes.* New York: Rosen Publishing Group, 2003.

Rappoport, Ken. *Tim Duncan: Star Forward.* Berkeley Heights, NJ: Enslow Publishers, 2000.

Stewart, Mark. *Tim Duncan: Tower of Power.* Brookfield, CT: Millbrook Press, 1999.

Thornley, Stew. *Super Sports Star Tim Duncan.* Berkeley Heights, NJ: Enslow Publishers, 2001.

Torres, John Albert. *Sports Great Tim Duncan.* Berkeley Heights, NJ: Enslow Publishers, 2002.

WEBSITES

Sports Illustrated.com

http://sportsillustrated.cnn.com/basketball

The online partner to the magazine provides access to articles on Tim's many basketball games with the NBA.

SlamDuncan.com

www.slamduncan.com

Tim's official Web site is packed with information about Tim, his team, and the foundation he runs with his wife, along with personal diary entries for fans.

NBA.com

www.nba.com

The official site of the National Basketball Association features articles on the current developments in professional basketball, links to teams and players, and an archive of past game recaps.

USA Basketball.com

www.usabasketball.com

The ultimate source for the latest news and stats on Team USA, this site also includes tons of facts about the players and coaches.

INDEX

Providence College, 14

R

Robinson, David, 43–51, 57,
    60, 62–64, 67–68, 71,
    79–80, 83, 86, 88, 92,
    95–96
Rodman, Dennis, 48

S

Sampson, Ralph, 50
San Antonio Children's
    Shelter, 74
San Antonio Spurs, 42–56,
    57–73, 77–93, 97
Scott, Byron, 89
Seattle Sonics, 79–81
Smith, Charles, 43
Smith, Dean, 24
Smith, Joe, 26, 29–30
Sports Illustrated, 64, 95–96
Sprewell, Latrell, 58, 62–63
Spurs Foundation, 54
Stackhouse, Jerry, 16, 26
St. Dunstan's Episcopal
    High School, 8–10, 15
Stern, David, 36, 42, 93
Street and Smith's, 16

T

Team USA, 64–65, 68,
    93–94
Tim Duncan Foundation,
    73–74, 76
Tomjanovich, Rudy, 49
Turner, Ted, 20
Twardzik, Dave, 29–30

U

United States Naval
    Academy, 45
United Way, 54
University of Delaware, 14
University of Hartford, 14
University of North Carolina
    Tar Heels, 1, 16,
    24–25, 27–28
Utah Jazz, 53, 56

V

Van Gundy, 63
Van Horn, Keith, 38
Virginia Military Institute, 33

Vitale, Dick, 21

W

Wake Forest University
    Demon Deacons, 1–3,
    12–20, 22–24, 26–40
Wallace, Rasheed, 16,
    25–26, 28–30
Washington Bullets, 29
Washington Wizards, 29
West, Jerry, 25
Wise, Mike, 59
Wofford College, 38
Wright, Sharone, 19